SOUL PRINTS

A COLLECTION OF POEMS, LETTERS AND ESSAYS

Helen White Wolf

Inspiring Voices®
A Service of Guideposts

Inspiring Voices books may be ordered through booksellers or by contacting:

Inspiring Voices
1663 Liberty Drive
Bloomington, IN 47403
www.inspiringvoices.com
1-(866) 697-5313

Because of the dynamic nature of the Internet, any web addresses or links contained in this book may have changed since publication and may no longer be valid. The views expressed in this work are solely those of the author and do not necessarily reflect the views of the publisher, and the publisher hereby disclaims any responsibility for them.

Any people depicted in stock imagery provided by Thinkstock are models, and such images are being used for illustrative purposes only.

Certain stock imagery © Thinkstock.

ISBN: 978-1-4624-0204-5 (sc)
ISBN: 978-1-4624-0203-8 (e)

Library of Congress Control Number: 2012941967

Printed in the United States of America

Inspiring Voices rev. date: 07/24/2012

CONTENTS

A Gesture of Gratitude. ix
Introduction xi
Soul Prints xiii

Part 1   Sunshine and Angel 1

    1. Star Mate. 2
    2. Background for Poem. 3
    3. Star Mate 5
    4. Sunshine 6
    5. This Is Sunshine 7
    6. Bubby's Letter of Love 9
    7. Puppies 10
    8. Angel. 11
    9. Remembering the Beauty. 12
   10. How Do I Say Good-Bye? 13
   11. My Precious Sunshine. 14
   12. Sweet, Gentle Angel 15

Part 2   Nature and Whimsical. 17

    1. Desiray. 18
    2. Grandparent Tree's Voice 19
    3. Whispers 20
    4. My Rainbow 21
    5. Butterflies and Fireflies 22
    6. Cloud Paintings 23
    7. Rain 24
    8. A Visit from Dragonfly 25
    9. Grandfather Sun 26
   10. My Visitors. 27
   11. Gobble, Gobble 28
   12. Father Sky 29
   13. Mercury in Retrograde 30

Part 3   Introspective 33

    1. Connected 34
    2. Wisdom 35
    3. Dance 36
    4. Many Lives 37
    5. Lessons 38
    6. Beware 39
    7. Manners 40
    8. The Dark and the Light 41
    9. Walk Your Talk 42
  10. Serenity 43
  11. Birth 44
  12. In Harm's Way 45
  13. Time 46
  14. Complete the Circle 47
  15. Give Back 48
  16. Trust 49
  17. Do No Harm 50
  18. Listen with Heart 51
  19. More, More, More 52
  20. It's Not Your Call 53
  21. Honorable 54
  22. Darkness 55

Part 4   People 57

    1. Joan 58
    2. My Firstborn 59
    3. A Prayer for My Son's Marriage 60
    4. My Son's Birthday 61
    5. Three's a Charm 62
    6. Alex's Poem 63
    7. Linda 64
    8. Winnie 65
    9. Dr. Jeffrey Langbein 66
  10. A True Friend 67
  11. Dolores 68
  12. My Lighthouse Jack 69
  13. Jack Mathias Noel 70
  14. Polly and Me 71
  15. Joel 72
  16. For Alice 73
  17. Loretta 74
  18. One Earth 75
  19. God Bless This Day 76

20. 1999 A Journey to Find Myself 77
21. Bear Heart 78
22. Joan's Necklace 79
23. Dear Dad 82

Part 5   My Personal Pieces 85

1. Who Are We? 86
2. Gotta Be Me 87
3. Glimpses 88
4. Wishes 89
5. Truth 90
6. Good-Byes 91
7. Beholder 92
8. Betrayal 93
9. Abundance 94
10. Advice 95
11. Anger 96
12. My Funeral 97
13. Let's Call It a Day 98
14. The Curse 99
15. Enough 100
16. Thanks 101
17. Spirit 102
18. Helping 103
19. The Nest 104
20. Being Human 106

Part 6   God/Angels/Spirit 109

1. Angels 110
2. Hello from Heaven 111
3. Mika'il 112
4. Raphael 113
5. Ariel's Nectar 114
6. Gabriel 115
7. The Heavens 116
8. The Four Winds 117
9. To the Fullest Extent of the Soul 118
10. Miracles 119
11. Blessings 120
12. Angel Spirit Guides 121
13. A Letter to God 122
14. My Daily Prayer 123
15. What Is Prayer? 124
16. Message from Spirit 125

17. The Soul 126
18. Stone People 128
19. Mother's Day Weekend 131
20. Ancient Knowledge 134
21. Introduction to Reiki 136
22. My Chakras 140
23. Chakras 141
24. Healthy Lifestyle 142
25. Letter to Brian and Matt 143

A Tale to Tell 145

A Gesture of Gratitude

This letter is to thank the ones who made this book possible. They start with Sister Corinthia, my sixth-grade teacher at St. Bedes. You taught me to be aware of details, to focus, and then to put the words on paper. You supported and guided me during a very vulnerable time of my life. I think of you often and regret that I never told you how you changed my life. Thank you for teaching me the passion of wanting to learn and be alive.

Next, I'd like to send a shout out to Dr. Langbein. I can't count the times you told me to write my story. You've always made me feel important enough to listen to. In today's world, it's hard to find people who care a lot. I love how your head always follows your heart. Maybe someday you could write a medical manual on how to treat your patients with the utmost respect, which is what you've always shown me.

Then there's Winnie Troxel. You've given me support in spades. When I wanted to stop writing, you kept telling me to keep going and not throw my pieces out. You listened to my pieces with such an empathic ear, and you gave me much-needed praises. You always let me be me, without judgment on your part. You've been instrumental in my evolution for this last decade.

This part is to Linda Hampson. I know you don't want the public admiration I am giving you. That's all the more reason—you deserve it. You talked me into the computer, and then you taught me the basic tools I needed to create this book. You gave me supplies to keep the work going. You cared so much for me, Angel, and Sunshine, during the hardest times of our lives. I feel you own this book as much as I do. If anything ever happens to me, the rights to this book are yours, with my gratitude.

If it weren't for Ryan Stracci, a lot of my basic survival needs would not have been supplied. When people take it for granted that they have food, they tend to forget that others need help getting theirs. Ryan was there to help when my family was not. My life was dependent on him, and he's actually kept me alive to do my soul's work here. We have learned many soul lessons together, especially forgiveness.

The last person I'd like to thank is Polly Flanagan. After each piece was written, she was a sounding board. It was honored by being read out loud in her home. She was never too busy to honor each and every piece I presented to her. We are very different people, but she treated all my pieces with honor and respect.

Thanks to all of you, in each unique way that you helped me and supported me while I created this piece of art. I know that heaven looks down on each of you with gratitude too.

—Helen White Wolf

INTRODUCTION

This collection of my poems, letters, and mini-essays all have purpose and clear
intention.
This world is too complicated and overdone.
I want to leave something behind of value—true value—coming from the soul, my
spirit, and my experiences.
I made my pieces as simple as possible, direct and easy to read.
I hope to connect with those readers needing honesty from the heart and soul.

God bless all who read these,

Helen White Wolf

SOUL PRINTS

Soul prints is a collection of my private reflections,
Of my soul's personal journey here on Mother Earth,
Of my many experiences and my personal connections,
Of my multilayered being, my beliefs, and all their worth.

This beautiful collection takes form in many ways:
From sweet love and laughter it will change to sad tears,
But all will come from honesty, reflecting different days
Of living humanly, not wanting judgment from my peers.

My intentions come from sharing in an imperfect place,
Hoping that the various pieces, with so much diversity,
Will reach out in this dimension, without a need to race,
Simmer, digest, and finally resonate with many a new face.

All I ask of you is to hold, in all your head and heart,
One hundred percent compassion, and you will play the perfect part!

Helen White Wolf

Part 1

Sunshine and Angel

I've chosen Sunshine and Angel to start this book.
They were on Mother Earth when I started to write.
It started with Sunshine's cancer; I wrote his life book.
I didn't think I'd survive, but I tried with all my might!

I wasn't a writer, a poet, or an author, but I could speak.
So I took my pen in hand and did what he deserved.
I started at the beginning; I knew I couldn't be meek.
It really hurt; he was dying; I was totally unnerved!

After his book, the poems birthed and created new life.
Now Angel was living her last year but by my side;
As I wrote and wrote, she supported my pain and strife,
And now they watch me from heaven, and in them I confide!

Now I want the collection all compiled in one book,
To go out on a limb and let the world see
All of my heart and what makes up me!

Helen White Wolf

STAR MATE

I am you, and you are me.
Let this unfold, and let this be.
We will dance till the dawn,
So shall you see: I am you and you are me.

From the heavens above and the earth below,
I am you, and you are me.
From the beginning of time,
Your heart has been mine; I am you, and you are me.

The way will unfold if you just let it be.
I am you, and you are me.
The path will open; the skies will clear.
Just keep in the faith, my beloved dear,
For I am you, and you are me.

Together we'll be through eternity; I am you, and you are me.
The star in the heavens and in your heart
Are one and the same; don't let them part.
For I am you, and you are me.
And that's all you ever need to see.

Dedicated to Sunshine, my special star!

Helen White Wolf

And the Holy Spirit

BACKGROUND FOR POEM

I don't normally set up a poem with a background story. My poems are short, sweet, to the point, and very simple. This particular poem deserves to be honored with the truth of how my soul set this up, without my ego's control. Five months after the death of Sunshine (my beautiful golden retriever), I started writing a collection of poems. Well, at least I thought that was the start. I started with my poem titled, "Sunshine." That poem unlocked my artistic expression as a poet, and within eleven months, I had written seventy-four pieces. Now, I've never taken complete ownership of my pieces. Anyone who knows me will tell you I sit in a sacred place with angels when I write. I always state my poems are a cooperative effort with those divine beings. I never take full credit, because I believe in talking truthfully and honoring anyone involved.

It is now seventeen months since Sunshine left me. We went through a long, ten-month ordeal of his oral cancer before he passed away. In his last months, we would frequently wake at 4:00 a.m. A lot of those experiences were followed by dreams. One particular dream I had was that two golden retrievers were sitting by my bed. The dream spooked me; I woke and saw Sunshine sitting at attention and staring at me. He was at the bottom of the bed looking at me, precisely where the retrievers had sat in the dream. I knew instantly they were his genetic parents and weren't just in the dream. I knew their spirits were there protecting us and waiting for him to return to spirit. I came to the conclusion that angels were visiting us every morning at 4:00 a.m. while we slept. I knew their energy was so strong it would wake us up.

Last night, I had a dream that Sunshine and his mate, Angel (still living with me), had been stolen. In the dream, I had come home and found the door open, and they were missing. My thoughts in the dream were that someone would harm them. That uncomfortable feeling woke me, and I didn't go back to sleep for quite a while. Later, I fell asleep again and had another dream. In this dream, Sunshine was at the top of a street. He was just standing and looking at me. I called to him, and he ran right to me. Then Angel and Sunshine hopped in a car with me. I woke up and said out loud, "Thank you, Sunshine." I felt good after this dream. I knew he was with me and telling me he was okay in heaven. He still visits me while I sleep.

Today I read a story from Guideposts. The story is titled, "An Angel with the Power of Prayer." In the story, the author speaks of waking at 4:00 a.m. to an Angelic visit. I am very grateful that she told her story, and I'm not the only one who experiences these 4:00 a.m. visits. This is how my day started today. A few hours later in the morning, I was outside, and a beautiful woodpecker came and stayed for a while. I went to get my book *Animal Speak* to look up woodpecker. When I got done reading about the woodpecker, I noticed some papers inside the front cover. To my surprise, it was a poem I had written while Sunshine was alive. I had forgotten I wrote it because I was so consumed by his cancer and my grief. I never gave the poem a title. Currently, I always write the title first and then the poem. I remember when I wrote the poem. It was four months before Sunshine's death, and he was sitting right next to me on the back porch. I put it in the book that day and had not seen it for twenty months.

Today, with the help of the angels, I realize that this poem was written by my soul to be the first poem in the book, and I was destined to write poetry with angelic help.

I know, without a doubt, that angels (including Sunshine) were with me all night and today, setting this story up. There's nothing that could get me to change my belief. That's my story, and I'm sticking to it! With the story now being told, I am ready to title my poem:

STAR MATE

Thanks, Sunshine and all the angels for being with me all night and today.

Love,

Helen White Wolf

SUNSHINE

My baby, my love, my sweet, dear little dove,
Away you did fly, above and beyond
To a magical, mystical place full of love.

Your broken-down body is now pure light,
Shiny, mended, looking like new,
Laughing, playing, and taking on flight.

You took my heart with you, tethered a bit.
Part of it melted, broken in half,
The other part happy to know you are fit.

My head still remembers the beauty you are,
Your cute little habits, adorable smile.
At times my heart hurts that you are so far.

I'm jealous of heaven, 'cause now it has you.
The angels so honored and lucky
To bask in your presence, and laugh at you too.

Don't forget me, my love; save me a spot.
Make sure it's warm and real close.
Make sure all the angels guard it a lot.

Helen White Wolf

THIS IS SUNSHINE

He is my love; he was here for almost eleven years, and the most perfect years they were. He was a master beyond human comprehension. He knew respect and honor without being taught.

He came here to help my soul. He came here as an advanced healer from an evolved place that I don't even know. He knew how to meditate instinctually. He had a pureness that I've never experienced with any being in this lifetime; I've met thousands.

Words will never express or convey who he was. The great news is my heart knows and completely understands. The greater news is I was privileged to be graced with his presence and love for those blessed years.

He incarnated in this life as a dog: a beautiful, sweet golden retriever. Yet he was so far evolved beyond any human I've encountered. By the time he showed me he was ready to go back to spirit, I was convinced he wasn't always a dog. And by this time, I knew he was my master teacher with an old, huge soul. The trick here is I need to remember him as a dog. That was the role he chose for my experience in this life, but my heart will deeply know the truth: he was more human than me. I'll have to wait for my return to spirit for the whole story of who he is. Meanwhile I will be grateful with the memories of him as Sunshine, my loving golden retriever.

Happy trails, until we meet again, my sweet love.

Helen White Wolf

Sunshine, January 21, 1999 – October 27, 2009

You are my heart forever and ever and ever.
No one will ever take your place.

Bubby's Letter of Love

Bubby,

I love you, and I miss you more than I could ever describe. A woman who proclaims to be a spiritual teacher recently told me I had to let you go and your picture didn't need to be on my main screen. Sweetie heart, it's been only six months, and my heart switches from fond, happy memories to sad missing-you days. It just depends on the day, and there's nothing wrong with any feelings I have for you. No one gets to tell me how I'm supposed to feel and that I have to let you go. That's abuse of power to me and very disrespectful. It's my heart, and I'm going to honor and respect it, with all its ups and downs. I'm not hurting anyone, so there's nothing wrong with my feelings. I love you and I miss you, and no one anywhere is going to change that.

As far as letting you go … well, that's never going to happen. You will be my love for eternity. You are the sweetest, kindest, most beautiful spirit I know, regardless of where you are. And one thing I know about you: you would never give me instructions on how to feel. You taught me how to unconditionally accept another being's feelings, 'cause you are a true master. Every day there will be a mixture of happy miss-you feelings, and I'm proud to say that. I'm not changing for anyone; you're worth every feeling I have. And I will never tell other people how to feel; I will listen and respect that it's their heart and they get to use it their way. As long as they're not abusing or harming someone else, they deserve to be respected. I go out of my way to make people feel comfortable, and I'm going to start going out of my way to make me feel comfortable too. It's been a long, hard life; I'm dealing with too much illness and suffering. I'm not going to stab myself in the heart to allow someone's ego to overshadow me.

You understand my heart, just like I understand your heart. If I was in spirit and you needed me, I'd be there for as long as you needed me, and you can bank on that. There's no time limit in my book. I will always be connected to you. We were awesome together in this life and always will be. I don't need to justify or explain this to anyone. You were my love, are my love, and always will be my love.

Thank you for always being there for me. I know how great our spirits are together, and our love will outlast any unsolicited opinion.

Forever and ever, I am yours.

Love,

Mommy

Helen White Wolf

PUPPIES

Puppies are cute to look at.
Adorable fur balls, they are
Always available for a chat,
Always near, and never too far.

Loyal and ever so faithful,
Willing to share your time.
Never a moment that's dull,
Attentive at a drop of a dime.

To all who will love them,
No question, they love back,
While treating you like a gem.
Kisses and hugs you'll never lack.

If you're their lucky companion,
Blessed with them at your side,
Days will be filled with tons of fun,
And with them you can always confide.

They'll also take in your tales of woe,
Licking your tears and never say, "*No.*"

Helen White Wolf

ANGEL

You're a sweet, pretty girl, my blonde pup,
A golden retriever, through and through,
A bit on the plump side, and stubborn too.

After thirteen years, your tail still wags.
You move a bit slower, still at my side.
A big eater, your appetite won't subside.

You've come along way, and loyal still;
Friendly and gentle to all you meet,
Even though it's harder to get on your feet.

You always let me know when I go out,
You'll miss me, but you will wait
For my return, and our destined fate.

Every morning, you're eager to rise,
Greet the new day, to listen to me
Dictate the chores, while loving you'll be.

Helen White Wolf

Remembering the Beauty

Oh, how I forgot, with all that has come about, from ups and downs,
Leading me down a dark ridden path, creating continual frowns.
First came the loss of my physical health, once awesomely strong,
Willing to conquer all sorts of tasks—while singing a song.

Next came the loss of a good-paying job and all that I held dear.
How would I make it day to day and not buy into the fear?
What would I do, where could I turn, I'd always done it alone.
The anger did rise, the tears did flow, I didn't want to turn to stone.

Depression set in, my mind a mess, my emotions pushed way too far.
Now I was feeling, was life worth living, and that became life's par.
The meds that followed created more problems, and on it went,
Soaring to heights I couldn't handle and didn't know how to vent.

The thoughts and emotions caused too much strife in my life,
Tension and stress so bad, you could not cut it with a good knife.
I was losing my children one by one, from every possible reason;
Then came the day, the horrible day, the death of my cherished son.

How could I go on day to day, without my sweet, shining light?
Everything drained, taken away, where could I find the fight?
To get up each day, make the motions, and try to take care of me,
To remember my love and all he gave and what he wanted for me.

Well, it would have to be simple, and yet a huge task, to move on,
Fake the feelings, get out of bed, and eventually face a new dawn.
I would have to remember all of my son's love, joy, and beauty,
Embrace my new life, looking at it, as he would feel and see.

I will do it for you, my love,

Helen White Wolf

How Do I Say Good-Bye?

My sweet retriever pup, here we do sit,
For this is our last month that we will share.
I named you Angel, and it really fit;
You lived up to the energy, always full of care.

For close to a decade, many losses we endured,
Faithful at my side, you've tried to console.
But now, my dear love, your health can't be cured.
How will my heart mend; it's taking its toll.

You're the last one left; it's just been you and me.
I'm trying so hard to be strong, but it's a façade.
Pretending it's okay; there's been denial, you see.
That I am okay with sending you back to God.

My heart is so torn; our bodies are weak.
We lean on each other as we suffer our pain.
You need my help; relief you do seek.
How do I let you go and still stay sane?

Forgive me, my friend, if I've kept you too long.
It hasn't been easy, a sorrowful song.
I can't stand the thought of being alone
Still in my own pain; this is so wrong.

Helen White Wolf

MY PRECIOUS SUNSHINE

Special, sweet Sunshine, today's been exactly two years
Since your soul did leave me and started new tears.

Unconditional love definitely was your main goal,
Showering my entire being, touching right to my soul.

Nurturing you were, straight through to my core.
You always knew how to comfort me, that's for sure.

Sweet were your steps as you followed me around,
Wanting to always be with me, even out on the town.

Honorable was a trait you knew how to wear well,
A great role model for everyone, and this I will tell.

Inquisitive with innocence, chomping at the bit,
Running about, exploring, but you knew when to sit.

Noble was your character, magnificent in stature,
Beautiful to gaze at, with a loving heart inside you.

Exceptional and excellent in every one of your ways;
I was more than blessed to live with you for all of those days!

I still miss you and love you and thank you, sweet dove!

Helen White Wolf

SWEET, GENTLE ANGEL

Angelic you were in body; your name always fit.
Today, seven months ago, you went back to spirit.
Every day in remembrance, a sacred candle is lit!

Nonviolent you were, an ambassador of peace;
Aphrodite would have been proud to call you niece.
An icon of beauty, in all your totality, not just one piece!

Graceful from your head right down to your tail,
Your personality so mellow, a sweet girly-girl, never a male.
No matter what I would ask of you, you would never fail!

Exquisite in every single facet of all that you were,
Your adorable growling was more like a content purr,
That you were just the happiest pup, with lots of blond fur!

Lovely, Lovely, Lovely, I can't say it enough;
You knew how to play nice, and you didn't get too rough,
For gentleness was your only goal; you just weren't tough!

Sweetheart, I'll never forget your unselfish deed of
Extra innings, awesome support, and all the love!!!

You earned the Purple Heart, sweetie. I love you!!!

Helen White Wolf

PART 2

NATURE AND WHIMSICAL

The following group of poems were a joy to write.
I love being outside and the feeling of connection.
On my back porch, I would take in Nature's delight,
Sit with my Acer computer and express inspiration.

There are lots of huge trees, plus oodles of green,
Rabbits, squirrels, bird families, and even a skunk.
The beauty's just awesome, making me feel serene;
The clouds seem to speak like a soft-spoken monk.

The stillness and beauty fill my being with love,
And the words start to flow, with a life of their own.
I go into a surreal zone, channel energy from above,
Let the expressions unfold, with a sweet, sweet tone.

I am never disappointed when the writing is done;
I read over the poem and realize, I sure had fun!!!

Helen White Wolf

DESIRAY

You are the tree that has come to me,
Planted by the birds, secretly and sacredly.
You had a reason; you had a purpose
To teach me your knowledge, without any fuss.

Well, I sit here below you, puzzled a bit;
Don't know how to do this; can't throw a fit.
I've been told to listen; can't use my ears.
Frustration, my dear, could turn into tears.

I look up at your beauty, leaves so green.
Puzzled, bewildered; are we really a team?
If we are connected, spirit and soul,
This should be easy and not take its toll.

The birds do love you; they sing every day,
Sitting on your branches, with lots to say,
Their hearts so filled, their voices so sweet,
I just sit, watch them, and listen to them tweet.

Well, I can't do that, so I will stand, hug your trunk,
Sense your love, drink in your nectar, stay out of the funk,
Feel your veins pulse, your heart beating for me,
Grateful as ever, oh, you taught me, *I see.*

Thank you, my tree.

Helen White Wolf

GRANDPARENT TREE'S VOICE

My family has been here for millions of years.
Way before you came, we stood in this place.
We stood still, peaceful, strong; we created no harm.
We saw the beauty of Mother Earth, and love on her face.

We are one with our Mother; our roots run deep.
We take no more than needed; the balance we keep.
We've watched you for too long, the damage you do.
The problem we've noticed; the caretakers are few.

This is the day I've called you to listen.
To shed the old ways, step up, and to glisten.
Stay still, peaceful, strong, and silent to boot.
My words are important; they are your new suit.

I'll be your strength, your support, your guide.
We'll reconnect; I'm here at your side.
Tell me your problems; in me, you'll confide.
I'll keep you grounded from those who have lied.

My roots, still connected to our Mother Earth.
Yours have been severed; you feel no worth.
You feel disconnected and lost in your way.
Grab onto my trunk; listen to what I say:

Your blood is my blood; we're one and the same.
Let's get on the same page, create a new game.
Take care of ourselves, and our Mother, too.
Every action counts; this concept's not new.

Gentleness is needed everywhere you go.
Be wise with your touch; always make it so!!!

Helen White Wolf

WHISPERS

The winds do comest forth and beckon to play
As they gently touch the chimes, making them sway,
Rustling through the trees, as if to sweetly say,
We are here; walk among us; if you choose, you may.

We will not harm you; we do crave your touch,
Connection, warm wishes, good intentions, and such.
You've been so busy, haven't been with us much.
Trust us, we've missed you; we promise not to clutch.

A gentle song we will sing you, simple at best,
Using all of our friends, who will call us their guest.
The leaves as they as they reach out, but not to test,
To complement and whistle and of course, to jest.

Gifts we do bring you, from your dear old friend.
The universe so large, remembers you when it can.
Fills us with warmth, gives us strength, love to lend
To your lonely heart, allowing it to mend.

Please walk among us, with arms open wide.
Embrace us, our old friend; turn a new tide.
We won't dare leave you, loyal at your side,
Calming and soothing, an honor to abide.

Helen White Wolf

My Rainbow

A rainbow has many colors, seven to be precise;
At least that's my belief at the current time,
And with that information, I feel fine.

Sometimes it's single; sometimes it's double;
Depends on variables and on God's hand
And where you're standing, precisely on land.

The sun and rain work in combination
As the rainbow reflects the water and light,
Creating a picture of awesome delight.

I enjoy a good painting as much as the next,
Especially when it fills the whole sky,
Taking my breath, releasing a sigh.

The rainbow's a symbol of many who see
That there's always beauty, no matter what
You're going through; with that, there's no but.

The rainbow's always a blessing to me,
And the loveliest sight to see.

Helen White Wolf

BUTTERFLIES AND FIREFLIES

They both are filled with light.
One flies by day; one flies by night.
Either way, it's perfectly right.

The butterfly basks in the sun,
Flirting and dancing, second to none.
Watching her is exquisitely fun.

The firefly, in the moonlight, glows,
With his light twinkling, off he goes,
Finding his mate, avoiding his foes.

Both are sweet and very serene.
To harm them would be so mean.
Enjoy their beauty; don't be a fiend.

Take in their beauty; watch their flight.
Notice that they don't want to fight.
Bask in their love, while using your sight.

Fill your heart with their love,
Reflecting the peace of the dove.

Helen White Wolf

CLOUD PAINTINGS

Cloud paintings by the breath of angels—
Are they real or just imagination?
My belief is they're signs from heaven,
But some people look for justification.

They bring up the question of what is true,
Looking for holes to destroy the theory,
Criticizing up and down, in and out,
Over and under, making them weary.

Never finding closure or sure answers,
They turn to science, looking for fact,
Creating more questions and sure doubt,
Leaving them full of ego-bound tact.

So full of themselves and myopic vision,
Closed-minded, stressed, wanting control,
Struggling and stretching every idea,
Exhausting themselves, taking its toll.

Why don't they let down their guard?
Open their minds and their hearts,
Letting go easy, learning to breathe,
Allowing the angels to heal their hearts?

Helen White Wolf

RAIN

Well, you've come to visit today;
It's been a long-awaited pleasure.
For weeks and weeks, it's been dry,
So very hot, with things starting to fry.

The heat's been completely unbearable,
Keeping everyone cooler inside.
The plants and the grass, all have turned brown,
Wilting and drooping, showing a frown.

The birds can't find water to drink.
All of the critters are searching for food.
Some trees look more like it's fall,
With their leaves turning color, starting to fall.

Most humans seeking shelter, or a cool pool;
Activities outside, avoidance the choice.
It's midway through summer; where's our green?
At the end of this season, will green be seen?

Well, you're here today; "more, more," I say!

Helen White Wolf

A Visit from Dragonfly

Today after reciting my Buddhist mantras,
A dragonfly, with all its beauty, did visit me.
It's been years since a visit, allowing me to see
Deep within my soul.

I did some research, to find some meanings
That would reach out to me and resonate,
Tickle my spirit, lift my soul, and show me fate
That he was meant for me.

I was surprised Japan was dragonfly island,
That the samurai would decorate his armor
With its likeness, praying for a victory tour,
Filling him with courage and success.

Native Americans consider it a messenger,
From another soul, and that's just fine.
After a grueling week, I needed a sign
Of joy and light to come my way!

Thanks for your beauty.

Helen White Wolf

GRANDFATHER SUN

It's a cloudy day, and yet I feel you,
Your rays, hidden in the darkness,
Waiting for a break to peek through.

I need you; I so crave your light.
Will you whisper to the clouds?
Open for me, please, with all your might.

I know that they can hear you
And my prayer, at best;
Their answer, a gap, would kindly do.

It would help my aching frown
To completely turn around,
Fill my spirit and make a new sound.

I've been feeling much, much sorrow,
So low, too many regrets;
I crave your light today and tomorrow.

You always remind me there's new life,
To hang in here with faith,
To forge ahead and release the strife.

I miss you,

Helen White Wolf

MY VISITORS

Today is Easter Sunday, and I'm not alone.
My pups are with God, my companionship gone.
So I sit here in silence, not even on the phone.
The weather is great, so I can't find a wrong.

Family can't be bothered—too busy, don't care,
Their agenda so important, others have to wait.
Should I grieve, cry, get angry? Let it go; do I dare?
Knowing down the road, that they'll live their fate.

Well, as the old saying goes, their loss, my gain,
For in the stillness and silence, blessings have come.
Birds of different families are here to keep me sane,
Coming and going; short, sweet play dates, are some.

Lots of small, shiny crows; their cousins, blue jays,
The doves and the cardinals, sparrows, and more,
The most beautiful redheaded flicker, I must say,
To the largest of raven, and the hawk that did soar.

Last, but not least, the robin reminds me it's spring,
To take in the beauty and remember to sing.

Thank you, thank you, thank you.

Helen White Wolf

GOBBLE, GOBBLE

Hey, Tom Turkey,
Will you be my friend?
Walk down the road with me,
Right around the bend.
Let's give thanks to Great Spirit,
Just 'cause we can!

Let's breathe the fresh air
And take in the sights.
Bask in the wonder,
While we dance in the lights.
Being joyful and happy,
We don't need any fights!

We'll have our memories
At the end of the day.
Reflecting on the friendship
And all we did say.
Would you give me a hug,
And I'll be on my way!

Helen White Wolf

FATHER SKY

Father Sky, whether morning or night,
You're always such a wonderful sight.
Wish I had wings and the power of flight.

I'd soar in your beauty, in the light of the sun,
Higher than the mountains; sure would be fun.
When nightfall approached, I wouldn't be done.

I'd continue my journey under Grandmother Moon.
You'd know I was ecstatic, humming a musical tune;
Soon I'd be laughing and sounding just like a loon.

Well, now, I don't have wings, but one thing's for sure,
As a two- legged, I can still dream and be hopeful for
Continuing fun under your canopy as I laugh and I roar.

Helen White Wolf

Mercury in Retrograde

Mercury, Mercury, what's up with you?
Businesses in peril; things seem like a mess.
Don't know where to turn or what to do.
Can't make a move; haven't heard a yes.

Everybody's talking, not making any sense,
Trying to make plans, coming totally unglued,
Feeling like a bird perched on a fence;
Which way to fly, without getting sued.

Communications, travel, they're all a bust.
Frustration, no peace, becoming the norm.
Sanity I'm seeking; peace is a must
For me to attain in the middle of this storm.

"A few weeks," you say, "a few times a year
For total upheaval, shake things up a bit;
For change is a-comin', my sweet dear.
Have some faith in me; try not to throw a fit."

"It's always for the better, with love I do this.
You'll like me in the end and throw me a kiss."

Helen White Wolf

PART 3

INTROSPECTIVE

The next group of poems are well rounded indeed.
Many different topics, just thoughts that run deep;
Some may have antidotes that are meant to seed,
Open your soul more, in your consciousness to seep.

None are meant to offend, just meant to ponder.
Perhaps you're having an off day, looking for reason,
To make sense of things, wanting to feel a bit fonder,
Hoping your day flows more, with a better cohesion.

Maybe you've had a bad week, and you need some time,
A new insight to a dilemma, or just wanting validation;
You're searching for the perfect words, a simplistic rhyme,
A short, comforting piece, just like the warmth of the sun.

Hope you find one or two that maybe suit you,
Resonate with you, and of course, bring you peace too!

Helen White Wolf

CONNECTED

Connected are we, different and alike.
Big picture, small picture, we're all one;
Different sparks under the sun.

Connected are we, the dark and the light,
Positive and negative; takes all kinds,
With different perspectives, one big mind.

Connected are we, the black and the white,
Squares and circles, different directions,
Ups and downs, still one reflection.

Connected are we, on ground or in flight,
Some with two hands, others four paws;
The winged ones and ones with flaws.

Connected are we, whether loose or uptight,
Straight-laced and narrow, footloose and free,
Each perfect in their way, we can all see.

Connected are we; we all need not fight.
Let's celebrate our differences, hand in hand,
Each singing their tune, all part of one band.

Helen White Wolf

WISDOM

When do you get to consider yourself wise?
If wisdom isn't knowledge, it's application.
Then what comes first, the chicken or the egg?
Or is it complex, like multiplication?

If someone calls you smart, is that wise?
And what about the name dropper and his criteria?
Based on what were you evaluated?
What are his credentials? Is he really superior?

If you look inside, do you feel wise?
Is there enough knowledge to make that call?
What about your ego and even denial?
Allowing yourself to feel bigger, foolishly tall.

Would a wise person ponder all these questions
And even put themselves out there
For public humiliation, and even debate,
Strip themselves of ego, totally bare?

Of one thing I'm sure—wisdom's just a word.

Helen White Wolf

DANCE

Everywhere you look, there's a dance;
Everything in life has its own rhythm.
It always takes two to create a dance;
One moves forward; the other moves back.

The moonlight shines; the sea will respond;
The fuller she gets, the wilder the tides.
The sun sends his rays, of which plants are fond;
The warmer the day, the bigger the leaves.

A male bird sings a song; the female joins in.
A squirrel runs up a tree; his mate runs down.
A male wolf howls, and the female finds him.
All animals have rituals, and that includes us.

We're a bit more complicated, harder to read;
Our songs more sophisticated—too many notes.
We send mixed messages, trying so to lead,
Making the dance hard to follow and succeed.
Choose your partner carefully, whoever they be,
Whatever your dance, in what you choose to see.

Helen White Wolf

MANY LIVES

Past, present, future! How many do we get?
What is their purpose? How do we choose?
Should we believe? Did we get it right yet?
Can we go backward? Can we go forward?

All valid questions; where are the answers?
How can we prove they really exist?
Where is our memory; please tell me, sir,
How to retrieve it and then believe it.

Why do we choose our parents, their traits?
Limiting, bothering, and some enlightening.
Setting the ultimate tone to live out our fate;
Entangling good with the bad, like it or not.

What about our siblings? Who comes first?
Is there a lottery of who will come last?
Then the question, how many, is a curse?
What's the perfect number? Too many? Or none?

The most important questions of all,
Is it worth living? Who makes that call?

Helen White Wolf

LESSONS

In this complicated, full-of-conflict world,
Universal lessons are still the same.
From the beginning of time, so simple they are;
The concepts not inconceivable, also not far.

Since the industrial revolution, we've overdone,
Forgetting principles, so easy to learn.
If we just stick to basics, we can evolve;
Not creating problems that need to be solved.

They all start in heart, then follow the head,
So that our actions don't create harm.
Love steers you straight, keeps you in line,
So the goal for everyone could always feel fine.

If we start out each day with intentions to play,
With compassion, gentleness, patience in spades,
Forgiveness, sharing, helping much more,
Then to sweet, beautiful heights we will soar.

Understanding and nurturing, not to ignore.

Helen White Wolf

BEWARE

Beware of those

Who would give you advice.

Beware of those

Who will tell you of right.

Their long, lengthy tales

Of woe and of fright.

It's a sure guarantee,

You'll lose sleep this night.

So stay in your heart,

And trust in the light.

Helen White Wolf

MANNERS

Our current society has lost its soul and current values.
Boundaries no longer exist, causing unhealthy lives,
People bulldozing, trashing, and downright disrespect too;
Cell phones, computers, cameras, the likes, not just a few.

Seems like most act like children; can't find the adults.
Toys everywhere you turn, no limits in sight;
Children raising children, manners getting worse;
Impatience, rudeness, carelessness, and more. Oh, what a curse.

Listen to me; watch what I do. Oh, yeah, to hell with you.
I'm in a hurry, I want more, I don't want to be bored.
No one seems to care about the next one in line,
As long as they get what they want and they feel fine.

Yet that fineness they feel winds up so short-lived,
Leaving them empty, unhappy, and looking for trouble
To cause to another, for more short-lived entertainment;
Self-centered attention, with selfish attainment.

Call waiting, a form of selfish interruption, missing honor,
No consideration for the first or second party.
Cell phones with cameras, no one asking permission
To steal part of their soul, and massive exploitation.

Where are the solutions to reverse this trend?
Bring back common decency, the rudeness to *end*.

Helen White Wolf

THE DARK AND THE LIGHT

In these troubled times, things don't look good.
Mother Earth is seeming shaky;
Floods, tornados, tsunamis, many quakes,
Upheaval and rebellion seem like a should.

There's nowhere to turn, to escape the wrath;
No country has a waiver,
No continent immune; we're facing effects
Of what we created. *Look,* just do the math.

There's no turning back; it's cause and effect.
We ignored all the warnings,
Continued on our path; destruction seemed our goal,
Being ignorant, often topped with neglect.

Many humans on this planet made the call
To pull out of the darkness into light,
Change our habits, to much higher consciousness.
A path once ignored that led us to the fall.

Now that we've allowed the dark to rule,
How will we find the light and not be so cruel?

Helen White Wolf

WALK YOUR TALK

The spoken language between two individuals
Seems so easy, and offered so quickly.
I'll be there, I'll call you soon, I'll do this or that.
Time slips by, words do die, and that's that.

No one called, no one met, nothing got done.
It leaves you wondering, were you talking alone?
Time still continues, keeps ticking away;
Are you dreaming, wondering what may?

Might or might not happen; you were there.
Where were they and the promises made to you?
Your words were sacred and honored too,
But, now you ask, what are you to do?

Keep silent to avoid a potential feud;
Confront the offender, risking a terrible split.
Let's face the truth: it's a no win situation.
Keep true to yourself, honor your words,
And pray for lack of frustration!

Helen White Wolf

SERENITY

Love, peace, and happiness should be natural.
After all, you were born with those traits.
Then came experience, in every which way,
Creating fear, apprehension each day.

There were beliefs and thoughts imposed upon you,
You didn't ask for; regardless, they exist.
You wanted approval, so you bought right in.
Now you feel trapped; oh, what a sin.

What should you do? How should you feel?
Who should you believe? What's the right path?
So many people, and different schools of thought;
Which one is right for you, without being caught?!

What happened to your freedom and peace of mind?
Life's such a maze; maybe too many choices.
If it were simpler, would you feel serene?
Happiness returning, your perfect scene.

Serenity is perception; your peace is personal.
Be true to yourself; it's the only right way!
Please try to remember to honor what I say!

Helen White Wolf

BIRTH

So many species here on Mother Earth
Wonder where they came from; don't you?
All so different, a collage of amazement,
And seemingly so easy to reproduce, too!

Doesn't take much effort to conceive,
But then the work begins, the female's labor,
An agreement she made, God only knows when,
To create a child, just 'cause she can.

If all goes easy, it only takes months
To nurture and feed the baby within.
If there are complications, baby may not be born,
Leaving Mom feeling weak, not happy, but torn.

It's a huge responsibility to keep baby healthy,
But Mom gives it her all, no matter how hard.
Baby comes first, with her comfort on hold.
Will she get due gratitude, remains to be told.
Sure hope she gets it and is not treated cold!

Helen White Wolf

IN HARM'S WAY

I've spent the last year at everyone's mercy.
Bad health was an issue for too many years,
Learning to deal with too many limits,
Waiting for help, shedding a great deal of tears.

Everyone had their health; they took it for granted.
Their lives were busy, balanced with joy;
My life was deteriorating, creating more issues;
No one could hear me or heal me. Oh, boy.

I was trying my best not to bother anyone;
I wanted them happy, and I was a pain.
My life and my home became a great mess,
So I tried to handle things, not to complain.

That wasn't the answer; more problems arose.
I needed more help, but I was ashamed.
No one really understood, and always had advice,
To tell me what to do, like I should be tamed.

The outcome of this was denial or argument,
Bad advice, being taken advantage of too.
I've taken a bloodbath, financial and health;
My life really in jeopardy. Are you guilty too?

Helen White Wolf

TIME

We are born here on Earth, with bodies, movement,
With agendas and plans, and lessons to learn,
Much experience to acquire, possessions will be sent,
Each day slightly different, with energy to burn.

The days will go by, followed by weeks and then years,
Before you know it, a decade or two, or even more;
Time will be fickle: one day slow or changing gears,
To speeding by so quickly, no one knows for sure.

This is for certain: time never stops; it just goes on,
Without your permission, it plays its own tune.
It's impossible to control and destined to be gone;
Were the moments peaceful and not gone too soon?

Were the days filled with love, from near or far?
Was there any laughter, or maybe, even a frown,
Feelings of contentment or of raising the bar,
A sense of worthiness and wearing a crown?

And what will tomorrow bring, of this I will sing,
Only time will tell; hope it's heaven and not hell.

Helen White Wolf

COMPLETE THE CIRCLE

A couple of decades ago, I got a message.
In it, I was instructed to complete the circle
With my spirit, just starting to bloom.
I had no idea how to go about this.

Then mysterious things began to happen,
Things I could not explain. People showed up,
Strange books would appear, all timed just so,
As if it was already planned to fill my cup.

I felt like a pawn in a well-orchestrated plan,
A destiny of sorts, of which I would follow.
If I bucked the flow, I'd get stuck, frustrated,
Felt like I'd fallen down and could not go.

Then I learned my Native American heritage
Was all about circles, to open up, stay aware,
Feel and see the signs, while sensing spirit,
To live my predestined fate, if I do dare.
So now I challenge you:
How do you *complete the circle?*

Helen White Wolf

GIVE BACK

If you've been here, even just for a day,
You owe someone or something, in some way.
You wanted to be here, so you chose birth;
I'm sure your agenda was to feel mirth.

Now, what that meant to you was personal.
With that in mind, you chose a vehicle
To enter this world, to play out your plan,
Even if those around you were not your fan.

The first ones you owe are parents indeed;
Without them and God, there's no seed.
Whether you like it or not, it's universal sooth,
Good relations, bad relations, it's still the truth.

Along the way, you've encountered more debts
Of all your connections; so be honest, and let's
Look around, plus looking back, open our mind,
Reach out, try to give back; now's the time.

Try to remember, forgiveness is giving back.

Helen White Wolf

TRUST

Who can you trust? What can you trust?
Will your eyes guide you well, or even your ears?
Will your feelings steer you wrong, with fears?
Do you use all three; are they a must?

Can you trust someone one time, not the next?
Is he honest in business, dishonest in love?
Can you separate the two, keeping yourself above
All the pettiness and garbage, free from his nest?

This much I've learned, carving it in stone—
There's no separation; he's either honest or he's not.
Something in his soul, foul-smelling snot,
Infesting your spirit, feeling rotted and alone.

Next time you question, trust your own gut,
Not to give your trust lightly or easily so.
Make him earn it and earn it, to become your foe
A lesson well learned, and you won't feel like a nut.

Helen White Wolf

DO NO HARM

There's a school of thought, why we're on Earth:
It's the plane of lessons for God's evolution.
We were allowed to separate from the light,
To descend into darkness, no longer in flight.

The goal was simple: ultimately find our way back
To the greatest of love, the sweetness of breath.
The tenderness of touch, the honor of intention
To do no harm, I sincerely need to mention.

Awareness is the key of what we choose to do,
The words we say and, of course, our follow-through.
In order to achieve this, conscious thought we need
Of cause and effect, consequences indeed.

The problem that arose was the unhealthy ego;
It unfortunately wants control, at any expense.
Becoming very destructive, losing its sensitivity,
Giving itself priority, oblivious to others' longevity.

There's a popular saying, "no foul, no harm,"
Always said in hindsight, from the ego's point of view.
If you connect with my path, kindly use the foresight,
The intention, do no harm, so I can sleep at night.

Helen White Wolf

LISTEN WITH HEART

All through my years, I've noticed a theme:
People hear what they want, not what's said,
Picking and choosing the words that they like
For a personal agenda; we're no longer a team.

Seems to me, it's a question of control,
Making their agenda, your agenda.
Forget important words, putting you second,
Leaving you belittled, craving console.

The smallest of our words carry such might;
Deleting one or two changes our combined path,
Creates wounded feelings, and much distrust.
Restore deleted words, and we're back in light.

It takes pure intention, with clear focus
To honor each other, and our sacred words,
To discard our darkness, listen with our hearts,
Still our busy minds, listen without fuss.

To remember what was said is an honor indeed.

Helen White Wolf

MORE, MORE, MORE

What a time to be alive, a time to live or die.
Choices, choices, maybe too many for our good.
We want to own this; we want to do that.
Did we get lost in the quest and what we should?

We're bombarded with advertising and what to want.
Entertainment's a must—dull our senses, lose our way.
Losing our inherent values, no depth left to find.
Fill our souls with denial and destroy along the way!

Every single moment, opportunity does knock.
The freedom to choose, look inside, and reflect.
What should we choose, why go here, and do that?
Will we walk in harmony, with boundaries to detect?

Will we look to the right? Will we look to the left?
Will we look above us? Will we look beneath us?
Will we look where we're moving, what we left behind?
Will we value time, without making a fuss?

Can we make better choices, learn from our past?
Be satisfied with simplicity, or live our old ways,
Of more, more, more, for the rest of our days?

Helen White Wolf

IT'S NOT YOUR CALL

If it's not your body, if it's not your life,
Remember who owns it; respect is a must.
Refrain from opinion; don't create dust.

It's okay to watch, if you're invited.
Remember, leave space, room to breathe.
If arrogance calls you, it's time to leave.

You can lend a hand, if you're wanted.
Remember your talents; use proper tools,
Taking your time, not playing fools.

It's best to commit to thorough details.
Remember, mistakes often are costly.
They can cause harm, permanently.

It's best to review your original intentions.
Remember your actions—who they are for.
Keep them simple, not needing more.

From start to finish, try not to fall
Into the trap of, *it's not your call.*

Helen White Wolf

HONORABLE

Humbly walking through each day, with care,
Gently touching, hugging, kissing, if you dare.

Offering to reach out, with a helping hand,
For those in need; don't forget, include the land.

Nuturing with good intentions in your touch,
With the right amount, and not too much.

Occupy your own space; keep it clear and clean,
Sending out well wishes; try not to be mean.

Respectfully remembering the best manners,
Always try never to offend, 'cause it really matters.

Aspire to the high road, focusing to do no harm,
When someone needs a guide, offer your arm.

Believe with your heart, you can always improve,
Figure out better ways, then make the move.

Living honestly, in giving and receiving always,
Walking balance, boundaries, in all of your days.

Ethically remember compassion, forgiveness,
Understanding without judgment, then live your bliss.

Helen White Wolf

DARKNESS

How many times a day, month, or year
Do you feel the darkness, shed a tear?
Do you try to control it, go into denial
Repress it, suppress it, lock it in a file?

Where did it come from? Where will it go?
Will you surrender? Will you say no?
Does it control you? Do you control it,
Looking for light, or remain in its pit?

When it's overwhelming, it's hard to breathe;
So many things become a pet peeve.
Feels like you can't win, God hates you so.
Everything's so heavy, from head to toe.

Stuck in its grip, it's hard to see purpose,
Find your way out, without too much fuss.
This is the time—you must find the light;
Whatever it takes, be willing to fight.

Know deep inside you, help you do need.
It's okay to scream at heaven indeed.
To step up to the plate, follow your lead,
Treat you better; you're worth the plea.

Helen White Wolf

PART 4

PEOPLE

The following section was the hardest to complete.
Whether the person is now on Earth, or moved to spirit,
These pieces needed accuracy, a standard hard to meet.
I needed to respectfully honor them; the words had to fit.

The section starts with Joan, my most treasured friend;
She has moved on to Spirit, but I know she's not gone.
I sense her energy around, with the signs she does send,
I know she's now a spirit guide, but gentle, like a fawn!

The rest of the pieces will not have an order specified;
Each one is equal in value, and not one should stand out.
No one holds more importance; they all were by my side,
For every single person is totally unique without a doubt!

Please keep in mind, the reason I wrote about you
Was you got into my heart and shared my life too,
And now for eternity, I will feel divine love for you!

Helen White Wolf

JOAN

Words will not do her justice, but I will try
To describe who she was, before she did die.
She lived this life for sixty-six years,
Gave it her all, hid a lot of her fears.

She was sweet, kind, and gentle, and totally pure,
A giver, a helper, my friend, that's for sure.
She was eager to serve and lend a hand,
If you were blessed to meet her, you'd be a fan.

At your first meeting, she appeared small;
It wouldn't take long to know she was tall.
Her manners were impeccable, never selfish,
Extremely hard to anger; peace was her wish.

You were first on her agenda, with pureness of heart,
Always well wishes from the depths of her heart.
If you had a problem, an ear she would lend;
You could count yourself lucky if she was a friend.

She had a heart of gold; this is for sure.
It was an honor to love her;
I couldn't have asked for more.

Thanks, my angelic friend.

Helen White Wolf

MY FIRSTBORN

Fourteen hours of labor should have been a sign,
She was so determined to be born on her own time.
Eye color blue, hair color blond, she did look so fine,
The perfect high-boned, rosy cheeks; yep, she was mine!

She was born a Virgo, arriving Labor Day weekend;
She and I had quite the task to get her in this world.
Her holy birth took place, of the miracle God did send;
She had no fancy wings, but her soul seemed very old!

From the very start, she was determined and so bold,
She could pout, she could stomp her hands and feet,
She never liked to be alone, and she hated to be cold,
And when she learned to walk, she refused to take a seat!

As the years went by, she did grow and did mature;
She certainly wasn't a follower—she chose her own way,
Dressed to her own style, did her own thing, that's for sure,
And she still lives and learns her own way, to this very day!

Even if our journeys lead us a different way,
My heart will feel for her, every single day,
More love than I can say!!!

Helen White Wolf

A Prayer for My Son's Marriage

This is the holy, sacred day you embark into a new journey,
To depart from being as one, embracing now as two,
To venture into territory unknown, slightly scary and oh, so new,
So many choices ahead; how do you do your best?

You start with just one breath, one step, and just one prayer
That God fills your head and heart, and takes you by the hand,
Filling your moments with light, love, and bringing you new land,
Guiding you peacefully this day and whatever it will bring.

Pray each day for the highest good and best of all intentions,
For now you are totally responsible for you and for your bride;
Treat her well, with compassion, always wanting her at your side;
Be gentle with her, remembering every day to forgive her any faults.

Remember the innocence and sweetness you brought into this life;
Transfer those memories and emotions to her and your new life,
Always keeping in your mind, she is your chosen, cherished wife,
And then allow her to respect and love you from a giving heart.

Try to leave the past behind you, creating fresh, loving new starts,
Making room for clean slates and whatever the days will bring.
Then, as a result of all your work, you will hear the angels sing
The praises of your marriage and the love you hold so dear.

From the depth of my heart,

Your soul mother,

Helen White Wolf

MY SON'S BIRTHDAY

Thirty-three years ago, you decided to incarnate and to be born.
You chose blond hair, eyes of blue, a smile that filled my heart;
At that point, being innocent and tiny, I thought we'd never part,
The future so far ahead, not seeing us destined and to be scorned.

The years flew by, and before I knew it, baggage had accrued.
I did my best, with blood, sweat, and tears, to fulfill your needs;
Day to day, the burdens did grow, harder to avoid possible feuds,
Always praying deep inside me, I'd planted the appropriate seeds.

Now that you are a grown man, marching to your own tune,
I'm still praying for those seeds to take root and come into bloom,
For you to remember the truth of my heart, and forgive me soon
For all the wounds, inflicted and transpired, and yes, even gloom.

Meanwhile, with all due respect, I'll honor your chosen space;
With stillness and silence, I will sit, always with prayer in my heart,
Sending you love, honoring your lessons, at your own pace,
To remember your sweetness, generosity, and pureness of heart.

To dig deep in your soul, surrender, remember the good times—
The laughing, the playing, all that was done and given to you
From the best of intentions, giving you all of my dimes,
Doing everything I possibly could, always knowing I loved you.

Helen White Wolf

THREE'S A CHARM

It was Halloween; my last born chose conception.
A mystical time, with lots of supernatural energy;
From the ethers she came, as I partook in reception;
Right then, she showed God's power and what would be!

With a daughter and son already, she chose femininity,
To add to the dynamics, the many lessons left to learn,
Not only a female, but a feline to boot, a Leo in astrology,
Gifted to the hilt, strong-willed, with lots of energy to burn!

She wouldn't take a backseat; she always wore a crown,
Insisted on constant attention, and to be treated like royalty.
She had her ups and downs, could wear a smile and a frown;
She knew how to laugh, which would bring enjoyment to me!

Much like her older sister, she wouldn't follow the pack;
When she had something to say, she chose opposition;
Her ground she would stand, with no opinions to lack,
And now she's a young woman, in a big world of new kin.

No matter where she goes, no matter what her destiny,
She's imprinted my heart with love, and that will always be!

Helen White Wolf

ALEX'S POEM

Heaven only knows why we were born

On a special, appropriate day,

With lessons to learn, leaving us torn,

Feeling lost, and not knowing our way.

And even if you have nothing to say,

May blessings of God's will occur each day.

May God's light guard and guide you forever.

Helen White Wolf

LINDA

Light emanates from her heart; she lovingly cares,
Especially when she does what no one else dares.

Intelligence is her game, to use her common sense;
She's is very open-minded; she tries not to be dense.
If something's important, she won't be on the fence.

Nicely gentle and kind, just two of her qualities,
She's definitely a role model; she holds the keys.
'Cause it comes unconditionally, there's never fees.

Dazzling with beauty, from outward to inward,
She beams with light, looking upward and onward,
Always a peace seeker, doesn't want to use a sword.

A sweetheart, a delight, a joy to be around,
The most gracious of blessings to ever be found!!!

Helen White Wolf

WINNIE

Wise beyond her years, a true divine inspiration,
Having an empathic ear, and of course compassion.

Interesting to converse with, and always with charm
Combined with respect, and no intention to harm.

Noble in her character, wanting always the best,
She'll treat you with honor and knows when to jest.

Nice in abundant ways, more than meet the eye;
Her manners are appropriate, and that is no lie.

Introspective, intuitive, as a counselor should be;
I'm sure that most feel that way, and not just me.

Elegant in appearance, in speech, and in her space,
She likes to evolve, with each step, at a gentle pace.

Thank you for the blessing, being part of my life.

Helen White Wolf

DR. JEFFREY LANGBEIN

Well over two decades ago, I met a young doctor;
He had signed on with another doctor of mine.
My daughter was sick, needed attention for sure;
This was our first meeting, and such a good sign.

I had met a number of physicians before this man;
They all had their differences; none really stood out.
This gentleman was different, his heart in his hand;
I was sure he was a good soul, and I had no doubt.

When he moved his practice, a new group did form,
With qualified physicians, with whom he did bond,
I didn't question his intention; it felt like the norm,
For his good opinion, of which I always was fond.

Loyalty comes naturally, 'cause he is worth the visit,
To see his sincere smile, hear his comforting word,
Try his prescriptions, even when we tweak them to fit,
My strange, quirky genetics that don't follow the herd.

For many a year, he's been telling me to write.
Hope he enjoys this poem, that shows the light,
Of the wonderful physician; for me that's so right!!!

Helen White Wolf

A TRUE FRIEND

I've lived a great number of years,
And, yes, there've been many tears,
Incapacitation, loss of my gears.

I've known abuse, loss by the lots,
Confusion, frustration, anger, and grief,
Trauma after trauma; connect the dots.

To be all alone, help I did need.
Excuses, excuses; people were numb.
No one had time; I felt like a weed.

There's a young man, heart in his hand;
His life is busy, and he still makes time;
Always willing to help, whenever he can;
He cares if I live, to help me feel fine.

He doesn't owe me, yet he's still there,
Even when his own life doesn't seem fair.
His name is Ryan, if anyone does care.

There's lots of people who need a Ryan.
Please look around you; reach out if you can.

Helen White Wolf

DOLORES

Do you remember all you did right,
To make my life better, take on a new flight?

Of your many years, you struggled a lot;
Chores, many burdens, it seemed that you got.

Love was your goal, with no concrete map,
And many a day, onward you go, ready to rap.

Of your golden vision, a dream that you had,
For making my life better, and not so much bad.

Righting many a wrong—that you had to live,
Turning it around, with all you could possibly give.

Every decision was a battle in a world of wrong;
Finding new tools, looking for answers, you did long.

Say with all that you have, with love in your heart,
That you did your best to play the mother part.

Sending you love and gratitude and many blessings,

Helen White Wolf

My Lighthouse Jack

I lived in shadows at fourteen years of age;
My parents divorced, Mom had a new beau.
He was so kind and gentle, a new type of sage.
He stepped into my world with seeds to sow.

My life now changing, new ways to learn.
Who was this man? Where did he come from?
He was so different; his touch did not burn,
Quiet demeanor and charm, part of his sum.

The years did progress; he showed his skills
With love, music, magic, in his bag of tricks.
Much compassion to share; I didn't need pills.
He was a gentleman, one of Mom's best picks.

A beacon of light, showing and guiding the way
A well-weathered lighthouse, and wise to boot.
Peaceful, considerate, kind, gentle words to say;
The best of manners always he wears like a suit.

He's now my father; how grateful am I?
I'm extremely pleased; he's a wonderful guy!!!

Happy Father's Day

Helen White Wolf

JACK MATHIAS NOEL

I don't know when you'll get to read this, but at least it will be waiting for you when you're ready. The one thing I learned in the last year is there's no control on time and events. What God and our higher connection to God dictates will happen with or without our ego's approval. Unfortunately, that logic does not soothe our emotions and broken hearts. The heart's mending takes on its own unique, individual process, without rules. It is what it is, and all you and your support team can do is respect whatever journey the heart needs to take. As I told you before, your feelings are real and they're not wrong. They need to be honored. We are human and need to honor our emotional body. God seems to, because free will dictates that no one can change another person's feelings. I've watched for many years how people tell each other how to feel. I truly believe that just makes people hide their feelings to avoid ridicule, and then the heart doesn't get a chance to heal and move forward.

So, if I use Jack's love of music as a metaphor, I feel it would go like this:

There are many songs in the universe, and they all create *harmony and balance* for the universe to evolve. Humans continually need to sing their own individual songs, and those songs will be in constant transition, with high notes and low notes. Jack told me it wasn't a particular song he loved; it was the arrangement and what he created the song to sound like. His notes and arrangements could easily convey feelings without the spoken word. When he played the piano for me, I could hear the feelings. He could project the feelings of love, joy, anger, and a combination in just one arrangement. I never sat and judged whatever he played for me, because it was how he felt at any given moment. And the beauty of what he touched me with, was everything was created from love. When he played me a fearful arrangement, he didn't do it with judgment. It was from a loving being who allowed me to feel emotion through the beauty of music.

Jack always unconditionally was very gentle with me. He let my emotional expressions be heard. He was always supportive and loving, with an open heart and open mind. He had the biggest ears of any human I know—he knew how to listen. If the rest of the human race knew how to listen like him, we could have evolved to a very peaceful race eons ago. So I guess what I'm trying to convey now is he was a natural support team. And now that he can't do that, it's our turn to pick up the slack—to allow each other our true, authentic feelings, without judgment, and with compassionate acceptance of every given moment and every sudden turn our hearts will feel. It's the honorable thing to do, and I learned honoring the heart from a huge, wise old soul. That soul was Jack Mathias Noel, with his gentleness, joy, and giving nature.

God bless Jack always and all of us through this trying time. God bless us in how we will support one another from a gentle unconditional space in honoring each other's feelings. Hopefully we will keep harmony and balance. Hopefully we will remember how to create joyful arrangements, as our music master, Jack the Magician, taught us all. May God bless us all.

Helen White Wolf

POLLY AND ME

This morning I called Polly to ask for a favor,
Asking prayers to her angels and send them to me.
I wanted to write a poem, didn't say who for,
Surprise, Polly; I said it was special, and so it shall be.

Polly and me are neighbors across the street;
Within the last decade, our friendship has grown.
Who would have thought the birds do tweet,
Their lives so different, yet with comfort to loan.

Polly and me come from different generations;
With a thirty-year gap, what could we have in common?
There's caring and sharing, tipped with compassion,
Of course laughter, the good stories told under the sun!

Polly and me have completely different backgrounds,
From parents, to siblings, our lifestyles, the many choices.
We choose understanding to blend with our sounds,
Always striving for the harmony to reflect in our voices!

Polly and me know I have to move away,
With all optimism, I can currently say,
Even with the distance, the friendship will *stay*!

Helen White Wolf

JOEL

Joel was my neighbor for many a year,
An honorable man, not one to fear.
He loved to sing, and whistle a tune,
The loveliest voice over the moon.

Joel was a rare man, gentle at best,
Always a smile while working on his nest.
He loved a good joke, stories he told,
Making you laugh, fun fibs he could mold.

Joel loved his books, investing his time
In finding a good read, improving his mind.
His intentions and goals were always good,
Wanting to make you feel better, if he could.

Joel loved his family; they always came first,
Taking care of them, so they wouldn't thirst.
Joel's now in heaven, and this I do know,
He's earned his wings, and boy, do they glow!!!

Helen White Wolf

FOR ALICE

To heaven, she shall go,
A place that we don't know.
For when all is said and done,
Regrets, she will have none.

She will bask in heaven's glory,
That she lived, her life story.

And the love that's in her heart,
She will take with her, and not part,
From her earthly journey here,
Back to God, without a tear.

Surely, she'll be missed,
But with God, she will be kissed.

Helen White Wolf

LORETTA

Loretta, Loretta
You sweet little lamb,
Get better, get better,
As fast as you can.

The world needs your light;
Don't give up your fight.
Your heart is too pure,
Full of love, that's for sure.

People are praying;
Angels are too.
For our old friend
To recover—please do!

Helen White Wolf

ONE EARTH

One Earth is the name of a place that I go;
You might not care, and so you'll say, "So."
Well, that's why this poem has been writ;
I hope you'll take time to listen and sit.

There's a an acupuncturist, the owner indeed,
Who started this business and sowed a seed.
Her name is Evelynne, an honor to know,
Her intentions are sacred; she's giving it a go.

It only takes one visit to learn she is kind,
A conversation or two, you'll know she's a find!
Her heart is open, filled with optimum care;
You know you're in good hands, better than fair.

She's taken the time to give it her best,
To make you feel wanted, a welcome guest.
Her love is in the air; you can't mistake it;
It's unconditional; she's the right fit.

If you're looking for awesome, this is the place
To put your energy, a smile on your face.

Helen White Wolf

GOD BLESS THIS DAY

Hark! The herald Angels sing,
God bless this day.
As I hold this Angel pin
That was sent to me
By a very talented artist
Named Steven Lavaggi.

Hark! The herald Angels sing,
God bless this man.
The Angels must guide his hands,
Of this I am sure.
While he leaves his heart open,
His talents do soar.

Hark! The herald Angels sing,
God bless this day.
For the many creations,
And the blessings received,
For all the willing participants,
And all they will be!

Helen White Wolf

1999
A JOURNEY TO FIND MYSELF

I walked Mother Earth, here and there,
No particular destination,
Finding my journey go everywhere.

The beginning brought the classroom scene,
Bringing the distaste of rules and regulations,
Making me, again, feel like an outraged teen.

The spring gave birth to Sunshine and new healing,
A new teacher, a new way to communicate,
A new way to dialogue with my inner feeling.

The spring also brought feelings of romance.
Although this relationship did not bloom,
I learned to grow and dance a new dance.

The summer beckoned me to solitude.
Now was the time I had to face my darkest demons,
To gracefully free them, without a feud.

The fall produced a powerful, authentic medicine man.
I watched my children step into their own spirit.
I was feeling my deepest love again for the land.

The winter approached, with angels sprinkling love.
A channel singing forth a "parade of spirit,"
Ending my year with the peace of the dove.

God bless every spirit that shared a dance with me in 1999.

I love you all.

Helen White Wolf

BEAR HEART

A long time ago in an Indian village, there lived a very special man. He was a medicine man. He was named Bear Heart because of the goodness in his heart. The goodness was very strong and could not be broken. Great Spirit put it in his heart so he could help and heal the people and animals of his tribe.

He was always connected to Great Spirit. Every morning he offered prayers of thanks to Great Spirit. He also prayed for the wisdom to do good deeds, all through the day. Great Spirit never let him down and could always speak great words of wisdom through the love of Bear Heart.

Bear Heart spent his life being gentle to all of the two-legged and four-legged creatures, and the winged ones, and the water ones. He was always honest, kind, respectful, and helpful, and he never stole. He shared all that he had. He took great joy in always listening without interrupting his brothers and sisters in the tribe. He also had a very special gift of being able to hear the animals and the trees and the plants.

When you get the Indian name Bear Heart given to you, it is a great honor. It means that you have the same gifts from Great Spirit that were given to that special medicine man. All that Great Spirit asks is you use your gifts in a sacred manner to help Mother Earth, her children, animals, and plants. It all comes from your heart.

Helen White Wolf

JOAN'S NECKLACE

Joan and I had been friends for a couple of decades. We worked together, and we enjoyed each other's company. We started out as coworkers, but each year our friendship grew stronger and stronger. Joan knew I believed in reincarnation. I often told her I'd live a million lifetimes with her as a friend. She also knew I wouldn't say that to very many people, and it was true. This July 4 will be five years since Joan passed away from cancer. No one will ever convince me that Joan's spirit didn't choose freedom day on purpose. She was now free from all her pain and suffering. Joan was the most gentle, caring person you could ever meet. She was one in a million and had a pure heart of solid gold. I was truly blessed to have her as a friend.

I'll never forget the day she gave me the news. I went into work, and she asked me to speak in private. She started to cry. Joan wasn't one to cry in public; she always put on a good show. She was the person who always smiled and wanted to make you happy. She was so overwhelmed and just didn't know how to handle it. That was the day our friendship started down a new path. Previously, Joan had known I was studying my Native American spirituality. Here and there, we had talked about my passion for it. But now things were different; Joan was starting to ask spiritual questions of her own.

One day a friend of hers wanted to tell her something. Her friend had lost her teenage son in an accident. She told Joan that butterflies kept coming to her. Her friend was convinced it was her son and he was giving her a sign. Joan knew all my animals and critters had spiritual meanings. She asked me what the butterfly meant. I told her they stood for transformation. That it was a good sign he was okay in spirit.

When Joan's time was getting close, she chose a butterfly to be put on her memorial service pamphlet. She also chose the saying "Life is changed, not taken away." So for that reason, when a white butterfly shows up around me, I say, "Hi, Joan." At this point, you shouldn't be surprised to read that a big white butterfly is flying around me now. It's not just the butterfly that means Joan to me; it's also the daffodil. Joan used to give them to me, and they've been showing up a lot recently. That's how I knew it was time to write this story. I know we're writing this together—she in spirit and I in the physical plane. For those who don't believe this, I would ask you not to criticize and stop reading. This story is beautiful, and I'd like it to remain that way. I'm truly writing this story for people with open minds and hearts. Criticism was not the intention of this piece of work.

Well, with all this information I gave you, are you wondering where Joan's necklace comes in? When our journey shifted to a spiritual one, I tried to keep our energy positive, and I would give her gifts to keep her in God's light. Most of the gifts were angels. I would always tell her I was a pawn the angels used. I never had to look for her gifts; they would just show up. All I had to do was believe and feel God's love; the rest was a cakewalk.

One day I was in a mall. I was walking through and ran into someone I had been thinking about for a couple of weeks. I hadn't seen him in a year or more. He had previously moved away and just moved back into town. I knew that's where the magic started. We had a lovely conversation, and I then continued shopping. I ran across three silver necklaces of the artist Raphael's angel. I bought all three. I gave one to my sister, kept one for me, and gave one to Joan. When I went into work the next morning, I went straight to Joan. I explained how there were only three necklaces and I bought them all. I told her I knew it was Raphael's angel. I thought it was a good sign, because the Archangel Raphael means the "medicine of God." Joan loved it, as she did all her angel gifts.

Joan's mother was also ill and didn't live close. Joan would go on periodic trips to help her parents. Shortly after I gave her the necklace, she took one of her trips. Her mother needed to go to the hospital for some tests. Her mother wasn't functioning well physically or mentally. Joan didn't want her father to know she wasn't doing well. She didn't want him to worry about her and her mother. So Joan took her mother to the hospital. When she got there, she didn't know how to get her mother out of the car and into the building. She held onto the necklace and started praying for help. She told me her mother's mind became normal and her mother walked as if she hadn't any problems. She told me her mother was completely normal throughout the tests and walked easily back to the car. Then when she got into the car, she went back to a dysfunctional state. Joan was convinced it was because she held onto the necklace and prayed to the angels.

I never saw any necklaces like that again, until recently. It was around eight years ago when I gave her that necklace. I've been having my own health issues these past years and have many a difficult night. One night I couldn't sleep again, and I turned on the television. The Home Shopping Network was on, and there was Joan's necklace. It was even better, though. Joan's was made of silver, and this was silver on one side and gold on the other. The company that makes it is Michael Anthony. They're brothers, and I love their names. Archangel Michael's name means "he who is like God." And Saint Anthony is the saint of miracles. When Anthony talks about the jewelry, he always speaks of his faith. He surprised me once when he said angels guide him in what to design. That takes a lot of courage to say on national television.

It would have been enough to have just seen the necklace to give me some peace that night, but something else happened. Along with white butterflies and daffodils, cardinals are Joan's signs to me too. When Joan's cancer would get bad and she would have to go into the hospital, she would call me. She would ask me to say my prayers because it always made her feel better. A lot of the times when Joan called, a cardinal would show up and I would tell her it was back again. The night the necklace was on television, it was in the middle of the night. Anthony was talking about the necklace for about fifteen minutes. Right when the necklace came on, a cardinal started singing and sang until Anthony said his last words about the necklace. My jaw just dropped. The cardinal was quiet for the rest of the night.

There's nothing else to say but thanks. Thanks to Joan, thanks to Anthony, thanks to Michael Anthony Jewelry, thanks to HSN, thanks to the cardinal, thanks to the Angels and all who follow their guidance. I needed some peace and faith that night, and I was blessed with concrete signs of belief and faith.

Joan, I miss you.

Joan, I know you're around.

Joan, my thanks, as always.

Helen White Wolf

Dear Dad

Pat just brought you, on a surprise visit, to see me a couple of days ago. I'm writing this letter to be read out loud to you in spirit. The reason is because your ego and personality are not present anymore, but your soul can hear me. During our visit, you couldn't remember anything, so I had to read you my poems and stories. I knew your spirit and soul were present because of your enthusiastic, childlike responses. Jesus spoke of being childlike to know God again, and I could see this in your face.

Years ago, if I would speak of God's magic in the universe and unexplainable experiences, you would argue logic and science to death with me. Well, you didn't this time. You kept saying," Oh, *wow,*" in a very peaceful and joyful manner. The look on your face was worth its weight in gold. That's how I knew that this visit was very sacred and your soul was calling out to me. I know that your soul wanted to say good-bye and be at peace before you left Mother Earth and returned to God. Well, Dad, we had quite a lot of experiences here. There were positives and negatives. But I know, without a doubt, that even our negative experiences turned into positive energy. I know because they were lessons on forgiveness and compassion. I feel that Jesus's spiritual platform to humanity was about just that. I know that we didn't have to speak out loud, that we had learned forgiveness. It was a given and felt in our hearts and souls.

Dad, I have experienced many losses and deaths in the past few years, and you'd think I'd be a professional non-crier at this point. Even though I know you are in good hands with God, there is still sadness in my heart right now, because I'm still human and have a heart. I think you'd rather see me cry and still care about you than be strong and appear heartless. So the tears are mixed for you in sadness and happy for you to be with Jesus and the angels again. You enjoyed laughing a lot, so here's to all the times you lectured me not to cry; it's still not working, Dad. They are tears of love. And the love is not a temporary state; it will be for eternity, whether we are together or separated. The heart and soul do not know time and space, so you can count on my love for you. I don't think the heart and soul have limits either, so I'm sending the love that is limitless and unconditional. I know you very well, Dad, and I know that wherever you are and whatever you're doing, you are wishing me the best and sending your love unconditionally back to me. So with that, I will say thanks for the journey, with all its ups and downs and all the soulful love in the unspoken words and the stillness of God's presence between us.

The last thing I like to say to you is about blessings. We were discussing the Archangels in our last visit, so now I'd like to write a small prayer for you:

May Archangel Michael guard your spirit and soul;
May all your burdens be lifted, without a toll.
May Archangel Raphael bring healing to your heart,
'Cause you have to leave and may not want to part.

May Archangel Ariel surround and fill you with light,
Giving you the confidence you are in God's sight.
May Archangel Gabriel sound his trumpet in tune,
That you're entering heaven, and not too soon.

May all of the angels, regardless of their size,
Bless your holy spirit, because they are wise.
May all of the saints bow down to you now,
In remembering your end, how you said, "*wow.*"

God bless, Dad. Happy trails to you!

Helen White Wolf!

PART 5

MY PERSONAL PIECES

In the following pieces, I go into the depths of my heart.
It's been quite a long journey; I've been through a lot.
Most years were hard, with much abuse in the cart.
Would I relive the difficulties? I surely think *not!*

No matter what was thrown at me, I would endure,
Be it rape, or the beatings, or just downright abuse.
I had love, regardless of ignorance, that's for sure.
I would reach up to God and pray for a loving muse.

I haven't been perfect, with times of a lot of denial.
I've had my own lessons on self-love and such matters.
At times my head was spinning; I felt like I was senile,
Trying always to push forward, finding myself in tatters.

Enduring abuse, neglect, mistakes, all done to me,
I'm still pushing forward, with lots more to see,
With love in my heart, to be all I can be!

Helen White Wolf

WHO ARE WE?

There are so many roles we get to play—
Male and female, child to adult,
A collage of colors, different moods per day.

Some of us with two legs; some of us with four.
Lots of winged ones; don't forget tails.
Tall ones with branches, veggies, fruits, and more.

Those who walk the land, and swim the sea,
From skinny to heavy, small to tall,
You were meant to be you, and me to be me.

How did we get here, and where will we go?
Gliding, sliding, walking, or running,
Lots of talking, growling, and purring just so.

Constantly growing, changing our tune,
Feeling different passions, seeking our paths,
Reaching destinations, never too soon.

We are all spirits, originally the same,
Stars of Great Spirit, from whence we came.

Helen White Wolf

GOTTA BE ME

I believe in many lives and evolution
And to live my current life, as if I have one.
So I need balance of work and fun.

If I find imbalance, I need a solution
Of how to press forward, completely with ease,
Finding enjoyment, not being a tease.

Living loving energy, sometimes revolution,
Batten down the hatches, full speed ahead.
"Look out, she's here," they once said.

Coming and going, filled with infatuation,
Try a project here, some laughter there,
Maybe even the occasional fair.

What I like today, with total confirmation,
Might not feel the same overnight.
Tomorrow, I just might fly a kite.

Whatever I choose, I gotta be me.

Helen White Wolf

GLIMPSES

Another week goes by, and you will call.
A conversation starts, and we'll fall
Into a pattern you set eons ago—*gossip*,
Where you wind up judging, to state your tip.

After all, if you can put down another,
Makes you feel big. When you ask me to conquer,
Never really taking the time to reflect
If there's harm in the tone that you have set.

Your agenda has been honed for decades now.
You groomed me for loyalty, and it feels foul.
Allowing you to continue your negativity,
For me to adore you, and never be free.

Free from the stories that you invent
When you speak of another's life with ill intent,
Taking bits and pieces, twisting them around,
Making false statements, you've now found.

I want out of your tiny glimpses of what you see
And how you keep me prisoner. I want to be free.

I prefer to be of goodwill.

Helen White Wolf

WISHES

Wishes, I have a special three—
An agreement between
The universe and me.

It will take some big entities
With huge, kind hearts
And the magical touch of genies.

The web will need to be weaved
Through and through,
Me to be patient, and not peeved.

I need the angels to listen
And not to ignore,
Allowing my dreams to glisten.

I've waited so long, so hard
For the universal big dreamer
To send me my lucky card.

My love boomerangs outward,
And now is the time
For the return, bringing it inward.

Helen White Wolf

TRUTH

What is truth? Who can explain this theory?
Everywhere you turn, everyone has answers;
One says black, one says white, one says me.
I know it all, meaning you owe me a fee.

What you say, you think you're better than me.
Where have you been, what have you done
That elevates you to superior and me to dung?
Changes our lives, and a new story has begun.

Now what's the truth, the old story, new story?
An in-between story? An overall celestial story?
Who gets to dictate what's right and wrong?
And who's orchestrating the complete song?

Well, I'll tell you this: for my life to be bliss,
I will need to be my own conductor and captain
In navigating the stormy weather and the calm,
Making my own way and writing my psalm.

All I ask of you is to treat me with respect;
Honor me with your ears, eyes, and heart.
Try more to be silent; try more to be gentle.
Embrace me with understanding,
And you will always know *truth*!

Helen White Wolf

GOOD-BYES

Every journey has a beginning, middle, and end.
The beginning starts with a thought, then makes a choice;
The middle goes every which way, around every bend,
And before you know it, you're facing the end.

Where did it start? How did it go? Did you follow the flow?
Were you in tune? Did you swim under the moon?
Did you buck the old system or cave for a foe?
As you look back and reflect, did you travel and go?

To where your heart led you, what really felt right?
Or did you step back and freeze, afraid of the night?
When things didn't feel right, were you willing to fight
For the freedom of your life and your awesome sight?

Is your heart content? Is it all said and done?
With possibilities endless, more choices ahead,
Your head filled with visions, looks like there's more fun
Out there, around the bend, and everywhere under the sun.

Well, my friend, don't sit and wait; gather your things.
Don't worry 'bout me; I'll be all right, and still your friend.
I'd rather say good-bye while we feel like kings,
Knowing deep inside, with lots of pride, it's really *never the end*.

Helen White Wolf

BEHOLDER

How do you behold a question so dear
And near to my heart? You have to dig deep,
Far below the surface, feeling respect,
Honor, and the likes, put into gear.

The mind needs to be still, lips kept tight,
Refraining from opinion, only to watch
Your heart, filled with empathy,
A practice in being, no action in sight.

The best place to learn is surely outside,
Taking in the visions, while staying still,
Sensing the details of all you see,
Wishing peace to all, no turbulent tide.

What are you seeing? What do you hear?
The birds sing together, the trees stand still,
The bunnies frolic, and squirrels too,
Butterflies flutter, with dragonflies near.

In this sweet space, you are a beholder.
You can take this feeling to your favorite spot
As long as it's sacred, beholding you've got!

Helen White Wolf

BETRAYAL

Have you ever felt a good friend profess their love,
Then turn their back, stick in the blade, and twist?
To make things worse, involve another,
Give out your number while you're amidst!

You get a call from a stranger who knows your life,
And she decides she knows best, belittles you.
Talks down to you from her high horse,
At the same time, dishonors you, too!

She's decided to fix a problem and create a mess,
Never looking back at the wounds she left.
You're there bleeding, heart ripped to shreds.
Tears just won't stop; huge scars she's left!

Meanwhile, your so-called friend never sees offense,
Goes about her business, figures she's been right.
In giving out your number, no second thoughts;
If she's caused harm, a potential fight!

Just 'cause she's too scared to talk the truth
And face you with honor. Now she's left you to ponder,
Is she really a friend? Would love do this?
Should you go on or is this the end?

Denial's not fun!

Helen White Wolf

ABUNDANCE

My whole life, I've felt ripped off.
I've watched others have so much more;
I've tried to do good and work real hard,
Constantly give, until I was sore.

I wanted to know, why did God hate me?
I would push myself to painful extremes,
Treat everyone better than myself,
Sacrifice always, it seems.

As I got older, I wanted more,
Tried to find balance in give and take.
But my relations were already groomed;
A new effort they wouldn't make.

As I spoke up, they were quick to argue,
Constant reminders, I wasn't good enough.
They loved the guilt card, used it a lot,
Pushing me to have to act tough.

I wanted to be gentle, and kind, and receive
Abundantly the Golden Rule toward me.
Haven't seen it yet, but I paid the fee.
God, I'm still waiting; what about me?

Helen White Wolf

ADVICE

In all my years, I've listened to advice
From this person, that person, and the like.
Very little of it worked, solutions they claimed;
Most were illusions for personal gain.

Do this, do that, guaranteed to work;
Remove your pain, make your life better.
You'll be happier, healthier, and much wealthier.
Their hands in your pockets all the while.

Finances being drained, stress even worse,
Feeling like a fool, while trying to respect.
Aren't they professionals? They've been schooled.
They should know more. God, this is lame.

I heal this, I heal that, if you give me money.
I can surely help you, remove your pain,
Turn your life around; things will get better.
Leave your purse open; your finances I'll take.

I'll live the good life, while you get worse;
Your money I'll play with, laughing with joy.
Don't care how I'll hurt you, on every level;
I'm happy, well cared for, at your expense!
Really?

Helen White Wolf

ANGER

When you are small, until you are tall,
There's an energy out in the world.
It's overwhelming; don't want it to call.

It engulfs many people, maybe even you;
It's loud and obnoxious,
Addictive to watch and listen, too.

It's uncomfortable to hear it scream,
Rear its ugly head, do its thing.
It looks for a victim to make a team.

It's hard to avoid; fall prey to its power.
It's always lurking around the corner,
Ready to pounce and turn things sour.

It doesn't know patience; it's swift to wound.
Nothing's safe when in its path.
You pray for protection, and not too soon.

It's been named anger; I hate its wrath.
I don't like what it does or how it feels.
I just want peace and out of its path.

Helen White Wolf

MY FUNERAL

It's my body; it was my life and my death.
It bothers me when I see people at a funeral;
I've watched them weep, heard them speak
Words that sound to be, oh, so deep.

Were they there through the days when needed?
It seems to me, most here on this solemn day
Were nowhere to be found, but occasionally
Dropped in here, stopped by there, always busy.

My dear friend passed on several years ago.
I watched as her health declined for some time
Prior to her crossing. A drifter here, a drifter there
Would stop by, claiming lots of glory.

The truth be told, she wasn't dumb; she was aware
Of how they chose to let her go, abandon her
In her time of need, a time while she breathed,
In current need of support and company.

Now my time's here, and I do declare,
I know just how she felt, alone; support I need;
Don't put on a show; put out your hands
When I have crossed alone. Step out of your glory.
Let me rest in peace. With God I'm not alone.

Helen White Wolf

LET'S CALL IT A DAY

When all's said and done, let's call it a day.
You chose a path, while I went my way.
You said, *Do! Do! Do!* I said nay,
It's time for good-bye, and that's okay!

Let's call it a day when we disagree.
You're calling orders that don't suit me,
Trying to control, not letting me be,
Stating a vision, I just don't see!

Let's call it a day; we're not the same.
Our opinions differ; I'm not to blame.
I don't want the chaos that causes the shame;
That's part of the program, after you came!

Let's call it a day and throw in the towel;
When you throw a punch—unacceptable, foul.
I want some peace, and I want it now.
You want it to work; I just can't see how!

Your lessons are yours, I do dare say.
I finished mine; let's call it a day!
Let's call a truce; let's call it a day!

Helen White Wolf

THE CURSE

Winter approached, and I came along.
Did you really want me; never felt that way.
So much rage you were filled with,
Your screeching voice, such a bad song.

I never felt good enough all through the years;
I'd try and try, never seeming to please.
All your reminders; I couldn't measure up.
So many bad memories, filled with tears.

Day after day, year after year, I was wrong.
Nothing I did was ever right in your eyes.
Your criticism constant, from morning to night.
Gentleness I craved; I waited so long.

Your curse on me lingered in my life.
Everywhere I turned, everything I'd do,
Would never work out; I'd never get it right.
A long, hard life filled with strife.

I know I can't change you; it'll have to be me.
To look deep inside, seeing my own beauty.

Helen White Wolf

ENOUGH

You think when I say, "Enough is enough,"
Things should continue just as they are.
That's just not so; don't be so tough.

You think when I say, "I have enough,"
My supplies will last forever and ever,
So you can be careless and treat them rough.

You think when I say, "Please listen to me,"
My words aren't worthy to take the time
To hear the details, for they are the key.

You think when I say, "Your orders don't work,"
It's okay to ignore me, stay in denial,
Blow me off, treat me like a jerk.

You think when I say, "Can't take any more,"
If you give me more orders, magic appears
And mysteriously will open a door.

I'm already in enough pain; it hurts to endure.
Your denial and orders are causing more strife.
I've got to find sanity, that's for sure.

Helen White Wolf

THANKS

Thanks to the morning, and Grandfather Sun;
To the air that I breathe, may it be always clean.
Thanks to the rain clouds, bringing us fun,
Nurturing our Plants, so green can be seen.

Thanks to the waters, from shallow to deep,
To Grandmother Ocean, with lots of her magic.
Thanks to the beaches, the shells that they keep,
The sands and the pictures we make with a stick.

Thanks to the birds, on land and in flight,
The songs that they sing, the feathers they leave.
Thanks to the four-leggeds, their wondrous sight,
The insects, the spiders, the webs they do weave.

Thanks to the fire, for light and such warmth,
For the endless chores it helps us accomplish.
Thanks to the two-leggeds, their heart and warmth,
Also amphibians, and all different kinds of fish.

Thanks to Mother Earth, the home she supplies,
The love, nurturance; plus she never lies,
Just showing us beauty for us to form ties.

Helen White Wolf

SPIRIT

As I try to describe spirit, many ways do appear.
For spirit is unseen, a powerful energy at best.
It's feeling in my heart, precious thoughts I hold dear.
Divine inspiration lovingly I allow in as my guest.

Where does it originate? How does it communicate?
What sends the messages, and when do they come?
Will I keep mind and heart open, believe in my fate?
Refrain from judgment, see many signs, or just some!

Every moment, every day, every year does go by.
I am here on Mother Earth; I walk in body, in form,
Wondering where I will go, with whom form a tie.
Will I trust my guiding spirits or stay with the norm?

Spirit knows my heart and my truest of desire.
My prayers said every day go out into the ethers;
I know they are heard and spirit feels my fire.
I know I need to listen, hear guidance, the answers.

Move forward and upward, with joy along the way.
Spirit sharing my dreams, with good stuff to say!

Helen White Wolf

HELPING

This short essay is about my personal quandary. I've been here on Mother Earth for nearly fifty-five years now. I was taught to work hard, do my best, and never be lazy. The attributes that were mine naturally have been an open mind and an open heart, always wanting to help in any given situation, in any way that I can. I've used my eyes, my heart, my ears in awareness; I didn't need someone to tell me what needed to be done. I was convinced that all humans had a heart like me and if I used patience and gave them their space, they'd find their awareness, because it's common sense from the heart. Well, this idea hasn't panned out and come into light.

Instead I've encountered the opposite in general. People work and live next door to one another and use judgments instead of seeing what our brothers and sisters are truly in need of, for just basic survival. Unless they get huge accolades for a gesture, it seems it worthless to them to give an effort. Where are the common decency and simple gestures to turn this around?

Helen White Wolf

THE NEST

It's been almost two weeks since my sweet, gentle golden retriever Angel left me. She was fourteen years and three months old. She lived a long, good life for a dog. I could see her arthritis in her last years. I understood her limits, since I was also dealing with my own arthritis and health issues. I had many losses in this past decade. These difficulties included my job, finances, and one health problem after another. All of these added up to stress and suffering you wouldn't wish on anyone. And if these things weren't enough to endure and bear, there were relationship losses and death after death. There were so many judgments instead of compassion just about everywhere I turned. A lot of poor advice caused more health issues and stripped me financially. Help was so limited—family members were busy working and running around, and they had a million excuses why they couldn't help. Recently I heard the phrase, "In the essence of time." In other words, my problems aren't important enough to invest in?

Less than a one and a half years ago, I lost my other golden retriever, Sunshine. His story wasn't like Angel's. He had nasty oral cancer his last ten months. Believe me when I tell you, there were a million excuses to ignore us in our time of need. The help I got and desperately needed was so little and always squeezed into a small, rushing "window of time." Sunshine's last day was forced to convenience and a small amount of time. A relative, who begged me for him, said work and school were more important than being there for him. Yes, money and time took priority over the life and death of a loved one. The icing on the cake was that she texted, "Is it over?" I felt this beautiful boy deserved so much better. He would do and go anywhere you wanted, with the best enthusiasm you could ever imagine. I don't hold malice against her, but I will never agree with her not treating him more honorably. She lives in a culture where money and material possessions outrank the spirit of life. I really think she missed the boat on this one. Needless to say, we drifted apart because our values were so different.

A couple of things were different and better in Angel's death, but I still got that "inconvenient window of time" thrown in my face again. My questions are, why would you make anyone suffer more than he or she has already? And is this how you want to be treated? I presently still have all my own health, financial, and need issues that need to be solved. It is a great test of faith. I still believe wholeheartedly in God and angels and guides, but we're having some deep conversations these days. I can't figure out why I'm still alive and what my purpose is now. Living in an empty nest with overwhelming issues has led me to ask God:

What could I possibly have left to do for you?

I still have a lot of love in me, but I require love
in balance here. Could you find it in your heart
to send me the good stuff now?

I'm losing strength on all levels; could you lend
me some to walk in beauty here?

These are the big questions in my heart. There's never a lack of little questions throughout the days, either. It feels like I'm hanging on by a thread, and I don't want to lose the love in my heart. But the truth is, it feels like the light in my heart is starting to dim. I still go outside and watch the animals and birds. No matter how bad a day can get, they always find a way to make me smile. And then my heart lights up again.

Today the birds were really loud, and the commotion drew me outside. When I went out, I saw a squirrel building a nest in the apple tree. I thought Sunshine and Angel must be sending me a sign to build a new nest. I felt the nest is a sign of birth and new beginnings. I felt the apple tree is about bearing new fruit. I also saw a butterfly for the first time this year. The butterfly is about transformation; I could use some good health and circumstances. I'm praying with all my heart this isn't the end of this story, and I will get to write a follow-up story, full of God's blessings to share with like-minded humans. And with that being said, please, God, build me a new nest, with all the trimmings.

From the bottom of my heart,

Helen White Wolf

BEING HUMAN

A master teacher once said to me, "Three-quarters of you is evolving. You are well connected to your higher self and your soul, but you are not moving forward as human." That was difficult for me to embrace and understand. I've had quite the life. It was busy, and I had accomplished many difficult, diverse skills. No matter what was thrown in front of me, I endured and tried to learn from it, and I would move to new phases and acclimate as quickly as I could. I had done more in my life than most others I knew. I was always learning and trying to better myself. I was always searching for the ultimate truth to understand all the ugliness I had witnessed. All I really wanted was a better life filled with happiness and peace. So I would search and search for that so-called better world. But no matter how hard I searched, drama would always show up to undo any peace and happiness I had achieved. To me, peace represents perfection. I used my perception of peace and projected it out into the world, which became judgment. The judgment would then destroy my peace. And then I was told I wasn't evolving as human. Dear God, how much more should I do? What have I been doing wrong?

I was giving daily thought as to why my humanity wasn't evolving. So now this statement was becoming an obstacle in and of itself. It was becoming such a burden to figure it out, I was torturing myself. With all I had done in my life, how was I failing as human? I live the highest morals possible. I was always double-checking my intentions. And in this state of trying to live the highest of ideals, I have been setting myself up for failure and non-forgiveness toward myself. I was caught in a vicious cycle. If I was caught in this cycle, then I wasn't moving forward. So how do I move on?

I'm currently focusing on the letting-go part of the whole lesson. To be human is to experience anger, grief, disagreement, dislike, discomfort, and other negative thoughts and emotions. My goal as I see it is to allow myself the human experience, to be in the moment with it, and to avoid obsession and being swallowed up by it. To process this energy with as little judgment as possible, I let go within a reasonable amount of time and move forward to feeling better.

And then at the end of the day, I can still look up at Grandmother Moon and the stars with love and appreciation. With those intentions I would have happiness and peace every night, and those feelings would be there to greet Grandfather Sun in the morning.

But what if I couldn't let go every single day? Would that mean I was back to being a failure again? Would I be setting the bar too high for success?

Most importantly, would I be removing the human experience necessary for my evolution?

Maybe, just maybe there's absolutely no answer to this and no solution. Maybe if I stop looking for answers and solutions, I'll mistakenly find more happiness and peace, than I could ever imagine.

And maybe my thoughts on all of this are what make me so human. Maybe just the fact I'm willing to give time to my thoughts and expressing them is what makes me human. Maybe I already started evolving my humanity while I was writing this piece.

The only thing I'm sure of is I want my personal happiness and peace to outshine all else. Won't you join me in this prayer?

Do you wonder what makes you evolve as a *human being*?

Happy hunting!

Helen White Wolf

PART 6

GOD/ANGELS/SPIRIT

Last but not least, these pieces are profound;
They have not been written for any argument
Or for those who would use a disagreeable sound.
They come from belief, a belief that you're not bound.

Faith travels different roads. Thank God for free will;
It keeps this planet interesting, and all we achieve.
I pray we do this all in peace and it's not all uphill,
That we honor all that we live with and what we believe.

The intention of these sacred pieces is pure beauty,
To see and feel the innocence, the holiest of now,
To remember the upmost reverence, very respectfully,
To humbly walk our own path, with no harm or foul.

Please hold on to what resonates; let go of the rest.
Remember God does love you, and I wish you the best!

Helen White Wolf

ANGELS

Angels are universal, common in religions.
Sight unseen, a given they exist,
From mothers to daughters, fathers to sons,
The knowledge is passed to coexist.

What is their purpose? What do they do?
To better our lives, to bring us joy,
Not just for one being or the chosen few.
To create all sorts of miracles, oh, boy!

Always busy as beavers, they don't complain.
Protecting and gifting every day,
Their goal in our lives to keep us sane.
At night they listen to what we have to say.

Their hearts always open, their minds in gear,
Wings ready to spread, for comfort in deed,
To calm us down, to remove our fear,
To send us messages, and plant a good seed.

To guide us in the most loving ways,
Showing us beauty to fill our days.

Helen White Wolf

HELLO FROM HEAVEN

We are not far, actually quite near,
Though you can't see us, try not to fear.
We enter your thoughts, also your dreams,
We try to inspire and send you light beams.

We were your brothers and sisters,
Your mothers and fathers.
In lots of cases, a daughter, a son;
Some of us angels, to send you fun.

No matter who we are, we mean you no harm,
Whether with you in a city or out on a farm.
Our goal is your goal; love is the game.
Our goal is for beauty; yours is the same.

You make the choices of how that will be.
We try to help you; can't you see?
We honor your free will, a gift from God,
Sending you love, an occasional nod.

All that we ask is you do your best,
Then take a breath; we'll do the rest.

Helen White Wolf

MIKA'IL

Archangel Michael, this poem's for you, with help from spirit.
I pray I do good, to honor your presence, reflect on your traits.
In gratitude, I write; with humbleness in heart, I bow down to you.
As a human with flaws, I reach up to you, to show me what to do.

As the "Prince of Light" and "Who Is Like God," send me mercy
With your sword of light, for God only knows, I'm not always right.
With love in my heart, I start out the day, but decisions aren't simple;
This world, it's complexity, can get so dark and fester like a pimple.

In these times of negativity and of fright, I call the "Chief of Angels"
From seventh heaven, and the "Sons of Light," the "Warriors of God,"
To show us the way, to use our swords, made of words and wisdom,
Put down the harmful weapons, shake hands, and just let peace come.

In our flawed humanity, our dark moments, with all our mistakes,
Please burn away our darkness, filling us with purity and with light.
Removing lower energies, bring our spirits back to love and support
Fill us with patience, comfort, happiness, and confidence of a sort.

Guardian Angel of the nations, who never fell from grace,
Please send your choirs of virtues, your Angels of Mercy,
To guide, guard, protect, and shine light upon this space.
Help us do better, bringing a smile to God's face!

Thank you, Archangel Michael, for your love when I'm lost!

Helen White Wolf

RAPHAEL

Archangel Raphael, bringer of God's medicine,
I have so many wishes and lots more to do.
Alone, it's impossible; with you there's a chance
To travel a new path, move forward, sing and dance.

My body is limited; there must be new ways,
From your divine connection, with the holy powers.
Could you find it in your heart to hear my prayer,
Wrap your wings around me, bring me good care!

One of the Holy Seven, the keeper of wisdom,
The Angel of Providence, to all who seek wholeness,
I do call out to you; open many a new door,
For my spirit's yearning to take flight and soar!

I've carried way too many burdens, worried too much,
Pushed my body past its boundaries; boy, it's hurt.
I have nowhere else to turn; you're my last hope.
Heal my mind and heart; make my life easier to cope!

I have one last big dream from deep in my heart:
Please grant my wish and help me evolve,
From this unhealthy life, begin a new start!

Helen White Wolf

ARIEL'S NECTAR

Archangel Ariel, with the loveliest aura of pink,
Thanks for your great work and your energy,
For our Mother Earth and our personal link,
To all the inhabitants and the beauty we see.

Often we think we are alone in our good deeds.
We tend to forget you, behind the scene,
Getting what's needed and sowing the seeds,
For Earthly creation, and many a bean.

We take much for granted in all that is here,
Surrounding us, supporting us, helping us live.
While you send us love, we forget that you're near,
With godly protection, guidance, and all you give.

Never expecting a thank you or tip of the hat,
In response to your loving gifts and all that we got.
Our planet, our animals, vegetation, food to get fat,
Our experience, our pleasure, so much in the pot!

Even when we ignore you, you're still around,
Still sending us blessings, without a sound.
Once again, I say thanks, from this holy ground!

Helen White Wolf

GABRIEL

Archangel Gabriel, heaven's winged herald,
Bring me good news, brighten my sight.
I've been called to duty, pulled back in the fold,
To live a spiritual life, spread my wings in flight.

Your name means, "God is my strength."
I could use some now, if you've got some to spare;
Please blow your trumpet, notes stretched in length,
To manifest loving huge favors, if you do dare.

Mary and Joan of Arc trusted you so.
Faith was their strength; they followed your lead.
I could use a vision, something absolute to know,
A positive direction to follow, and a sturdy steed.

As the "Angel of Truth," who brings the gift of hope,
Please clear the confusion that I sometimes feel.
Lead me on a good path, so I don't feel like a dope.
Help my spirit and body remember you're real!

Keep me in your prayers; please visit my dreams.
Fill me with confidence, reinforcing my seams,
And give the help to connect with great teams.

Helen White Wolf

THE HEAVENS

From where did we come, before we were here?
Somewhere in space, far away, or near?
What does it look like? How does it feel?
Does it last forever? Is it a sealed deal?

Does it stay the same, or continually evolve?
Do we have control on our problems to solve?
How many souls exist, single or in groups?
Do we go at it alone, or connected in loops?

All valid questions; we all have a view.
I'm sure some ideas are old, and some very new.
Can we get along as we search our own mind,
Living out each day, not fearful of time?

To each soul, I'm sure, you must be true
To your own belief, what resonates with you.
With honor I'll listen and ponder your thought,
Staying open to what I originally sought.

Helen White Wolf

THE FOUR WINDS

The East Wind graces me with spirit and sunshine,
The eagle flying high with fire in his eyes.
Spring, birth from ashes to beauty, the day so kind,
Honoring the Archangel Ariel as she flies.

The South Wind graces me with water and emotions,
The wolf and God's heart, the mouse and God's sight.
The rains bringing clarity, growth, and childlike fun
Honoring the Archangel Gabriel, all her might.

The West Wind graces me with spirit of Mother Earth,
The bear, with all his strength and protection,
Fall, giving harvest, abundance, from Mother Earth,
Honoring the Archangel Raphael and introspection.

The North Wind graces me with winter and wisdom,
The owl and stillness, the buffalo and sweetness,
The North Star's direction, my guides as they come,
Honoring the Archangel Michael, all his greatness.

Great Spirit governs all, and to this we owe *thanks*.

Helen White Wolf

To the Fullest Extent of the Soul

In current times, we have old-value rules;
Through judgment and punishment with justification,
Voices say, "To the fullest extent of the law."
If in fact our souls did dictate, we'd remove the flaw.

In a loving state, we would be, no threatening tones;
We'd always wish well, from a gentle heart,
Open and willing, listening with compassionate ears,
Supportive, allowing each other to spill our tears.

Seeking healthy solutions, with all in agreement,
To the ultimate heights, our egos must climb.
No ulterior motives, nor manipulation, nor control,
But first things first. We'd need connection to soul.

Meaning love comes first, no foul, no harm,
Knowing each spirit is equal, deserving of good,
In all our experiences and wherever we go,
Even in our mistakes, and especially when we say no.

That, my friends, is heaven on earth, when living
To the fullest extent of the soul.

Helen White Wolf

MIRACLES

Lots of people think miracles are big,
And don't count, if insignificantly small.
Truth be told, all and every size counts,
'Cause little ones make the outcome big.

Would you rather have only one that's huge
Or continual, ongoing blessing to blessing,
Converting a rather dull life to fuller, joyful,
Smoother, and flowing, with a guided muse.

I think it's more fun to watch them all link,
Let a story unfold, and the journey continue,
Not know where you're going, so it doesn't end,
All the surprises uplift you, without a kink.

So you can surrender all of your dreams,
Letting them remind you, you're not in charge,
Lifting your burdens, and ease up your life
To get out of your head, release your schemes.

All that's then left is a thank you indeed.

Helen White Wolf

BLESSINGS

Many blessings to you and me,
Miracles for us to see.
In harmony, they must be
For us to remain free.

Balance in gifts for me and you,
Boundaries and respect too.
With gratitude, we will do
Lots of thanks, not just a few.

In all things, beauty we'll see;
Holding honor is the key,
And not just on bended knee,
Every step, sacred we'll be.

Each gift we get, we'll pass it on,
Sharing every new dawn,
Gentle and sweet, like a fawn,
The breath of life never gone.

We'll keep ourselves clean and clear,
Holding each other's heart so very near.

Helen White Wolf

ANGEL SPIRIT GUIDES

This is my story, my experience, and all true.
From early childhood I had different feelings,
Something words could never explain.
My mother called me crazy, not knowing what to do.

My grandmother was passing, an angel came to say.
I sat at my window, crying for my loss.
My mother came in, stating I was a fool,
Leaving me feeling stupid and wrong; oh, what a day!

The phone rang that minute; she left me to answer,
Only to return with the sorrowful news.
"That was the hospital. Granny has passed."
Teaching me to trust angels did have the answer.

To what was real, that humans didn't get!
I was only nine with a lifetime to live,
With thoughts, feelings, undoubting experience
To know angels exist, without solid proof yet!

Don't ever doubt; your heart knows the truth!

Helen White Wolf

A LETTER TO GOD

Dear God, I seem to have lost my way.
There was a time I felt you, all through the day.
Full of joy, feeling giddy, merry, and gay.
But now I've been listening to what others say!

It's not working for me, 'cause I've lost my piece,
Of calm and serene, the most ultimate feast.
Where I adored and enjoyed my inner great peace,
Where nothing disturbed me, not even a beast.

I used to walk with you, beauty in mind;
My agenda was simple—always try to be kind.
It wasn't always easy, at times hard to find.
The goal still remained; for this I did pine.

I would walk in my silence; I'd be aware
Of the beauty you created, far beyond fair.
I could feel your heart in me, when I did dare.
Those feelings now escape me; where is my care?

God, please hear me—I've lost my way.
Help me return to your beauty each day!

Love,

Helen White Wolf

MY DAILY PRAYER

I call to honor and thank the East. I recognize Archangels Ariel, Uriel, and Jophiel, spirit, fire, spring, eagle, phoenix, birth to rebirth, ashes to beauty, and my personal prayers. *A-Ho*

I call to honor and thank the South. I recognize Archangels Gabriel, Raziel, and Zadkiel, the mouse with God's vision, the wolf with God's heart, water for growth and cleansing of emotions, inner-child healing, and summer with childlike play and my personal dreams. *A-Ho*

I call to honor and thank the West. I recognize Great Brother Bear Spirit, Archangels Raphael and Sandalphon, St. Anthony with the angels of miracles, St. Francis with the angels of compassion and forgiveness, Mother Earth keeping me grounded, fall with harvest and abundance, and my personal goals. *A-Ho*

I call to honor and thank the North. I recognize Archangels Michael and Metatron, spirit guides (past, present, future; individual and collective), the North Star, the wise owl and buffalo, the north winds clearing the way, winter for healing on all levels, and my journey to wholeness. *A-Ho*

I call to honor and thank Great Spirit, God—maker of all that is seen and unseen. I recognize the heavens, universes, stars, planets, Archangels, angels, ascended masters, masters, guides, saints, divas, air spirits, land spirits, water spirits, Mother Earth, Father Sky, Grandfather Sun, and Grandmother Moon. From all these holy, sacred powers, I call for assistance with my personal journey. *A-Ho*

Helen White Wolf

WHAT IS PRAYER?

This is my belief and my journey and my path to walk. I have been blessed to hear my angel guides my whole life. They have always spoken truth, and I have never had a reason to disbelieve them; I have experienced the opposite from humans in self-serving conditions. So today I once again sit with them and allow them to guide me to truth.

They always instruct me to keep things simple and be direct, not to buy into ego games and ulterior motives, and to stay clear and clean so I can hear spiritual truth and live spiritual truth. And this is a form of prayer. Prayer is a place where one is in the state of being grateful and wishing well for all—the all being humans, animals, every creature, Mother Earth, the universes, and physical and nonphysical beings. If you're in that state, honor and pure intent with respect will be second nature every moment of the day. Kindly be conscious of well-wishes and deeds every moment, and stay in the state of prayer.

Helen White Wolf

MESSAGE FROM SPIRIT

A true leader knows and practices how to listen, follow, and trust. The obsessive need to constantly know the answers is a practice of ego control and manipulation. This practice is not that of a true spiritual leader or healer.

The wounded ego feels the need to control and manipulate to avoid pain. Humans cannot avoid pain. Pain is the way the body and spirit release and heal. It is unavoidable. The sooner a human recognizes and accepts this, the sooner the human becomes happy and joyful.

If the ego has all the answers, the spirit cannot stay in the moment. You cannot continually project into the future and experience the moment. Remember the journey is not about the destination; it is about "being in the moment." If the ego is constantly chattering about the future, then it is impossible to hear and sense the higher self and soul. In that deafness, one cannot reach the spirit's true destiny and goal.

Delete the need to "know," and walk the journey in peace. Each step will be presented at the perfect time and not before.

Accept this and remain in the stillness of God.

Helen White Wolf

THE SOUL

Sit still and trust God loves you through all your choices.

Angels were not created to be ego servants. Angels serve God. God is a higher vibration of love. Ego is a lower vibration, often consisting of manipulation, control, blame, revenge, separation, punishment, and fear. Love is compassion, understanding, forgiveness, and the constant desire to serve a higher purpose. It is a place of wisdom of how to help one another, not destroy one another.

When the lower energies of control and manipulation come into play, the ego is instantaneously separated from the beauty of God's love.

Angels exist to steer you in the direction of a higher energy level of God's love. If angels get caught up in the specifics of one's ego control issues, then the angels step out of the higher love vibration and are no longer serving God. They fall from grace and serve ego.

If one's ego is ready to raise its vibration to a loving, godly state, angels are ready, willing, and able to accommodate and complement the beautiful energy.

But to ask an angel to lower its loving state to petty ego wars of control is asking them to strip their wings and leave God. While angels serve with love, they would never ask another to strip their wings for them. So doesn't it seem contradictory for humans to ask angels to strip their wings and lower their vibrations to games of control?

Angels are not biased—they love all and see the good in all souls.

This is why they will not step into small quarrels. And while most humans believe that their small quarrels are huge problems, they are nuisances and create more problems in the grand scale of finding God's love in their hearts again. These control issues that they have with one another block their true connection to God.

Angels want to bring humans back to God, not create more barriers.

So angels, from a loving place of existence, wait patiently for a human's ego to replace control with peace and evolve into a natural place of love. Love will always know how to come to a place of healing one's heart, gently finding resolutions with all that exist, and a beautiful harmonic dance takes place.

Harmony and peace are love! Fear, control, manipulation, blame, revenge, separation (from God), and punishment are not harmonic and peaceful; therefore, they are not love; therefore, they are not God.

Finding your way back to God's heart is to let go of the human pettiness and to feel peace for all that breathe in God's beautiful creation.

If you focus on the beauty, you understand God and become wiser to the true purpose of your connection to God. This can take place only if you are willing to heal all the pain, fear, and hatred in your heart so you can feel God's love again.

In the end all goes back to God.

So how does humanity learn to be with God in body—so one does not need to die to feel the beauty again? Only wisdom from the heart will help you release all the pain so you can feel the peace of God again. And this happens when people learn to help one another again, instead of blaming and judging.

Angels will always be there to assist when the heart is open to receive in a noncontrolling environment.

Humans need to release the pain to feel the love and to dance harmoniously with God and the angels again. How will each person find a place of peaceful healing of their pain? Well, that is what creation and evolution are truly about—finding the beautiful solutions along the journey. Love, let go, and feel God again. It's the only answer to all questions. God is everywhere, and your heart is the compass and the connection. Let the ego's mental chatter step aside, and stay in your hearts.

Helen White Wolf

STONE PEOPLE

"A long time ago …" sounds corny, doesn't it? Well, sometimes it's the only way to start a story. So please laugh with me, and we'll start again.

A long time ago, I was interested in nighttime courses to learn and evolve. I decided to take a course called Urban Shaman. I loved my Native American guides and all I had been shown already. So I was interested to see if someone new could teach me something I hadn't already experienced. The professor was not of a Native American bloodline, so I was skeptical … in a healthy manner.

He didn't really impress me or teach me a lot. I seemed to get more from the interactions with my fellow students. I should have trusted my own guides, that they would once again show me truth. There was one particular class on letting the stone people call to you. He gave us instructions to go out into nature during the next week. We were supposed to be still and allow a special stone to call to us.

The week went along, and I didn't feel a pull anywhere. We were supposed to bring the stone to the next class. During the next class, we were going to take the stone into the woods and communicate with it. Toward the end of the week, I picked up a stone just in order to have one.

Two hours before I was supposed to be in class, I got violently ill. There was no reason for it to come on that suddenly or to be so incapacitating. I couldn't make class that night. So because I didn't have the experience, I didn't believe the teacher.

I knew that stone people had different energies to help humans. I had studied them for years and had quite a collection. During my studies, I had been interested in obtaining an obsidian stone, for grounding purposes. I didn't want a snowflake obsidian stone; they are quite common. I wanted a pure black one. I never seemed to run across one, and eventually I stopped looking.

Two years after I had taken the Urban Shaman class, I was shopping with my young daughter. We were in an urban mall and went into a science store. There were clearance boxes full of goods in the front of the store. My daughter was having the time of her life, just rifling through everything. I was watching her and then got a strange feeling. I walked away from her and headed to some drawers on the side of the store. I hadn't a clue as to why I was so drawn there. The drawers were open so you could see the merchandise. They were filled with boxes of stones from all over the globe. I looked down, and the first thing I saw was a solid black obsidian. I was in shock. Then I noticed it was from Mexico, and I've always wanted to go there. The stone was in the shape of a circle. I looked next to it, and there was another black obsidian, in the shape of a heart. I purchased the round one for me and the heart for my daughter. Both stones were predrilled to string for a necklace. They were very inexpensive, and I was thrilled with my purchases.

After we left the science store, we went to the food court. While my daughter was eating, I wanted to check my stone out. I noticed that the tag read, "rainbow obsidian," and I didn't know why. Then I wound up holding it, at a different angle, under the bright fluorescent lights. I noticed a rainbow heart in the middle of my round stone. The artist had carved angles on the top, to reflect an inner rainbow heart. I was so excited that my daughter's stone and mine were both rainbow hearts. This was just downright cool, and I couldn't ever have made it happen on my own. This took my guides, my daughter's guides, and the stone people calling to me. Boy, did I eat crow that day. It had taken only two years for my lesson to be complete. The lesson is always to trust that spirit will take you to truth.

That wasn't the end of the stone's experience for me. After the stone had such a powerful entrance into my life, I decided to wear it as a talisman. I wore it every day for protection. I always felt it protected my heart and soul. People were always drawn to it and would ask about it. I went to one class where there were students who studied crystals. They decided they knew more than the stone and my guides. They went into a negative space and told me it was too powerful for me to wear. I should point out that they had to ask what the stone was before they lectured me. That was one of my biggest lessons on how dangerous the ego can be. I figured out later that if I had removed it, they would have gained power over me. And that would have put me back into a place of not trusting spirit. So I continued to wear it, knowing it was one of the most beautiful gifts I ever had been given.

I wore it every day until my golden retriever got cancer. Then I was so concerned that he needed protection for his soul, I put it around his neck. He wore it every day until one day it was missing. I was frantic. I searched everywhere, inside and out. Over and over, I checked every inch. I was so afraid that it was in the yard and would get run over by the lawn mower. I found the cord but couldn't find the stone. He was waiting to die, and that's why I wanted his soul protected. I finally got exhausted and gave up, but I had a few choice words for spirit before I did give up. I then kept hearing the words, "by the door." There are three entrance doors to my home. I kept going to each one, back and forth, back and forth. Once again, exhausted, I gave up. I was really frustrated. Why did I keep hearing "by the door"? I just wanted some peace, so I started walking my prayer path in the backyard. My prayer path is a complete circle where I say prayers every day. I was getting calmer and figured I'd never see the stone again. I figured my prayers were going to have to guard him now. Just then I noticed something across the yard. It was under a lawn chair. I kept telling myself not to get my hopes up. When I got to the lawn chair, I looked under it, and there was the stone. I laughed because the lawn chair is *by the door*. Of course I apologized to spirit for my mistrust. After that incident I would periodically check the cord for a secure knot. My dog would routinely scratch himself and loosen the knot. I would then have to reinforce it.

A couple of months went by without a hitch; then one day the stone was missing again. I was so angry at myself for not checking it sooner. This time I couldn't find the stone or the cord. Yep, you guessed it: I was frantic again. This time I went for hours trying to find it and wasn't getting any clues as to its whereabouts. I wasn't going to get angry at spirit; I decided to just let it go. I knew my dog was very near his end and the stone wasn't going to save him. I decided to thank the stone and just say good-bye. There was a wizard movie on television, and I looked down and saw the stone and cord in front of the TV set. I promise you, it was not my imagination. I had been over that area many times, and it wasn't there. There was no one else in the house, so who could have moved it? I will always be convinced that angels, of some sort, put it there. He only lived a few weeks of life after that. I took the stone and placed in on a statue of Archangel Raphael (the medicine of God). After a few months of grieving, I started wearing it again. Yes, it's around my neck right now and will be until my death.

This story is powerful enough without anything else happening. But I neglected to tell a very important detail that happened the night before the stone first went missing. There was a movie on television. I had never seen it before and have never seen it since. I don't even know the name of the film. It was basically a Native American film. There was a Native American boy and a Caucasian girl. They met at an archeological dig site. The boy fell in love with the girl. He had given her a stone, and she wound up dying of cancer. He loved her so much and was there till the end. The movie paralleled my life in many ways, which are just too numerous for this story. But once again spirit showed me how they are always there. The magic and mystery of the universe just can't be explained. They can only be experienced and learned to be truth. The timing of this film and my life experience were so powerful.

Even though I don't know the name of the film, I'd like to shout out some thanks. Thanks to the writers, the actors, the director, the crew, the producers, and the PBS station that aired it that particular night. You see, I know their guides and higher selves hear me. So I send every soul who played a part in this story many prayers that blessings be bestowed upon them. I know in my heart that my beloved puppy does too. And if you're reading this story, may you be blessed with the unexplainable, cool magic of the universe. Remember, if you're skeptical while you read this, you'll eat crow down the road. You can't avoid it; it is what it is.

There's one last thing I'd like to mention. If you are an extremely skeptical person, try letting go a bit. My reasoning is you'll enjoy it and it will make your life easier. The experience is worth the belief.

Many blessings to you.

Helen White Wolf

MOTHER'S DAY WEEKEND

How do I start to tell a delightful story? Of course, at the beginning. I hope you have a smile on your face or chuckle a bit. That's what this story is all about. It's about smiles, good cheer, and laughter. And as always, it's about the magic of angels!

It was Saturday night, May 7, 2011, the night before Mother's Day. I decided to text a picture of a smiley face stuffed figure and a Happy Mother's Day text to Lorraine. She loves it when I send her inspirational pictures. She tells people the pictures are from her angel Helen. I wanted to make sure she got it when she woke up Sunday morning. I knew this would make her day. I shut the cell phone off and went to bed.

The next morning, Mother's Day, I decided to wear pink. I didn't have a reason, and I wasn't thinking about it. I put on pink pants and a white top with pink lettering, spelling ANGEL. In the morning I always go to the door and say prayers. This was a beautiful morning. It was sunny and warm, and it felt just wonderful. I noticed that the azalea out front had bloomed its first flowers;, they're pink. It was the first bloom of all my bushes and plants that year. I was so excited. I decided to call it "my fairies' Mother's Day gift." I clipped a small piece to put in a vase. After I got the vase, I decided to put it next to a small figurine of Mother Mary. Just then, my neighbor Polly knocked on the door. She had brought me a rose from church for Mother's Day. The rose was pink. She had debated what color to choose. She said she just had a feeling and chose pink. We laughed because of my fairy gift and my choice of clothing colors.

While Polly was visiting, I asked her to pick a card from my angel deck. I have four sets of angel cards from Hay House and Doreen Virtue. Polly had never seen the cards before. I looked down at the four boxes and didn't know which one to choose. I just reached down and grabbed a box. It was the Archangel deck of cards. I told her to shuffle them and pick one card. Her chosen card was the Archangel Jophiel, and its message was "clear your space." We laughed because she was cleaning her backyard that week. I told her that every time I gave the cards to someone, they were always accurate. I explained how I never touch the cards, so it's between the angel and them. Polly said, "Makes you wonder. No, it makes you feel good." Polly then left and went home. I then took the rose, cut it, and put it in a vase. Then I put it with Mother Mary, but I noticed it was too tall for her. I went and found a much smaller vase, and I had to cut the stem down a lot. I was feeling bad that I had cut so much of the stem and taken all the leaves off. Then I put it next to Mother Mary. It looked perfect, and I stopped feeling bad. I took another look at the arrangement and noticed something else. The figurine of Mary is holding a pink rose, and she is wearing a crown of pink roses. I just started laughing, as I knew this was all divinely guided. The angels always get me smiling and laughing with their antics. I tell Polly often that they tap on your shoulder and whisper thoughts and feelings to you. That's how they communicate with you, because they don't have bodies with voices.

After that, I thought Lorraine would like to hear this story. She likes my stories as much as the pictures I send her. She always tells me they make her feel good. She had replied to the smiley face picture with a message: "My angel Helen, I just love her. Dido back 2 u." I hadn't even eaten breakfast yet, but I wanted to tell her Polly's story. I called her, and she told me she had forwarded my smiley face message to a bunch of people. They all asked where she got it, and she told them from her angel Helen. I told her she was an angel, too, for forwarding it. That it was the gift that keeps on giving. I told her how I had gotten it from a dollar store. It amazed me how something so inexpensive was creating so much joy. It was the true spirit of "Pay it forward." As Polly said, "It makes you feel good." Isn't that what *love* really is?

As with all my stories, this would have been enough for a really good tale. But the angels weren't done playing, not by a long shot. The best part is none of it is fiction, and I could never have made all this up.

I always look forward to watching Joel Osteen's program on Sundays. They never disappoint me; they're always in sync with what I'm experiencing that week. It was program 499—Display Your Joy. He was talking about putting a smile on your face and being cheerful, that when you smile, it makes you feel better. I loved that he said it takes sixty-two muscles to frown and only twenty-six to smile. He was saying we were called to be the light of the world. The switch to turn the light on is your smile. Well, Joel, I did my part with a dollar smiley face text, by hitting a few buttons on a cell phone. I hope you're pleased and smiling. Just tell the angels if you have any more requests; I'm sure they'll get through to me. Truth be told, I feel they're always connected to all of us and we simultaneously pick up the same messages. I've always said that I'm just a pawn in their game of life—that they get me where they want me, and I just have to pay attention to my feelings. And then, all that's left is a good laugh.

I digressed a bit there. So please hang in there with me, and I'll get back to the story. A couple of hours went by, and I called my mother. She was talking, and I had her on the speakerphone. I picked up the Archangel deck, shuffled the cards, and picked one. I was shocked. It was another Archangel Jophiel card, but this message was about going outdoors. I looked at the picture of the Archangel Jophiel card, and she was holding a rose. In the picture, she not only holds a pink rose, but she is surrounded by them. Once again, I was laughing. I decided to take that card and a picture of my Mary arrangement to show Polly. When I went into her house, I saw she had cut her rose and a pink carnation down and put them in a Mother Mary figurine vase. The vase was given to her by her mother. The vase is also about the size of my figurine. We didn't know we were both cutting our rose the same height. And we didn't know we were making similar arrangements at the same time. The angels seemed to be having a really good time with us.

Once again, I'd be content to end the story at this point. But the angels aren't done with this quite yet. I later was curious to see the odds of both of us pulling the same Archangel. There are forty-five cards in the deck, so I divided the two cards by forty-five for the percentage. It read .0444,444. I have another book from Hay House. It's called *Angel Numbers* by Doreen Virtue and Lynnette Brown. I looked up 444, and it states there are *thousands* of angels surrounding you. You have a clear connection with the angelic realm and are an earth angel yourself. I laughed so hard, and I had to call Lorraine about her angel Helen. She was so glad I called when I did, because she was having some difficulties. Makes you wonder, doesn't it?

Well, I think it's a good story. It needs no embellishment, because the angels always orchestrate the perfect scenario. I would like to close with the following thought:

It's more fun to believe the angels love to play with you, than not to. I've noticed the more faith I have, the more proof I see. And the more I see, the more grateful I am. And with gratitude, it's easy to *smile*!!!

A big thanks to the spiritual angels.

And a big thanks to the earth angels.

Here's to smiling,

Helen White Wolf

ANCIENT KNOWLEDGE

I was given a suggestion to sit with a tree that the birds had planted by my house. I've always been extremely grateful for the strategic location that the birds and tree chose. She's right outside my living room window. In the summer, she helps cool the house with her leaves in bloom. She sheds her leaves in the fall, allowing warm sunlight to reach the house in winter. Last year I would hold onto her for comfort, while grieving my dog's battle with cancer.

I won't be able to stay in my house much longer, so now is the time to be with her and learn. I will miss her dearly, so I'm giving this my best shot. My dog Sunshine always knew she was special. He didn't lie down much outside; he loved to move around. When he did lie down, it was always under her. After his death, on his birthday, he sent me a sign. He got thirty robins to fill the tree in late January. It was totally quiet, and I didn't hear the robins fly in; I looked up, and there they were, still being totally quiet. I was so surprised and couldn't move for quite a while. I just said, "Thank you, Sunshine," and then I cried. As quietly as the robins flew in, they left. It was a once- in-a-lifetime experience, and I will always be grateful to Sunshine, my tree, and the robins. To this day, whenever a robin lands in my tree, I say thank you to Sunshine.

I started the story this way to give a background of how mystical and powerful this tree is. I talk to her, but until recently I didn't realize how to communicate with her. I have had so much thrown at me this past year, I'm finally just giving up my control issues. So now I'm meditating with her and allowing her to give me visions of her ancient knowledge.

She has started by showing me how all the tree roots use Mother Earth to send their energetic messages to each other. And at the same time, they send and receive their energetic messages through their branches. Their thoughts are similar to our thoughts, in that they send out intentions. She has shown me that ancient healers programmed healing information into the trees for future generations to retrieve. The trick is making sure you step out of your ego completely.

She has started teaching me how to breathe in sync with her. I sit and hold onto her until I'm completely still, and then I focus on my breathing. At first the breaths are circular and relaxed, and then she deepens them. You have to really let go and trust her. The in-breath is through the nose and extremely long. The out-breath is forceful, through the mouth, and also extremely long. At no time is my mind engaged. It is total experience and hard to explain. I have to let go of all thoughts and all feelings. I have to just *be* in the moment. When I let go of all human control issues, I then feel her energy surge through me.

It's my understanding that humans knew how to do this in the beginning of our existence. It was natural and commonplace. We didn't need a human teacher to instruct us. It's coded in our DNA. Our egos took such an unhealthy turn. While our egos suppressed our DNA coding, the trees stayed faithful that we would come back to communicating with them.

Our major block is that we want to put everything in human words. In order to connect with the trees and their beautiful energy, we must stop talking. Our egos have a tough time shutting off the chatter. That's why we can't sense the trees anymore. If we let go, we'll feel their wisdom again. They know what energy our spirits are in need of. If you hold onto a tree that resonates with you, you don't have to figure anything out. The energy is transferred through the silence and the love. If you think about it, when you envision something, it's wordless. You just see a picture, and you're okay with that. That's being in the moment; it's communicating without words. It's true connection. The trees have memories, just like we do. You just have to be quiet and let them show you the visions. You won't need words; you'll understand what you're seeing.

So ancient knowledge boils down to this: sit still, surrender, be totally quiet, let your senses of vision and body sensations surface, and let the tree fill you with unconditional loving energy. It's simple; don't let your ego step in and make a huge production out of it.

Love your tree, trust your tree, hold onto your tree.

Let your feet feel the tree's roots. Let your hands feel the tree's trunk. Let your heart feel the tree's loving energy. Let your spirit see the tree's memories. Let go of all expectations, stay in the moment, be grateful for the experience, and allow the tree to guide your connection with it. Remember, if you step out of the way, it will be the best experience.

Helen White Wolf

INTRODUCTION TO REIKI

Reiki is an ancient Japanese practice. It is spiritual and sacred, and it is treated with the utmost honor and respect. It has been passed down from master to student from ancient times to the present. It is a form of spiritual energy healing.

The student studies with a master for three different levels, with the master performing energetic attunements for each different level. After the third level the student can then go on for a master teacher certification.

The Reiki master is an instrument for the highest, purest energy from the universe to be passed through the master's body via the master's hands to the client.

Our spirits cannot be defined or measured scientifically or physically. They are composed of energetic thoughts and feelings. In order for the energy transfer to be of the highest, purest nature, Reiki practitioners must place their egos aside and learn to still their minds (quiet rambling thoughts) and personal feelings on any issues that could lead to a detrimental session. Learning to meditate on a daily basis keeps the mind still and your practice sacred, as it was originally intended to do.

Your practice needs to be kept sacred and honorable by using professional ethics and high standards. This is done by not repeating any personal information that is revealed during the session. If you choose to gossip about information you have acquired during a session, you've now stepped into your ego and you are no longer performing the sacred act of Reiki.

It's best to empty your mind and emotions before you start the session and at the end to keep respect for your client. You need to remain a clear conduit for your present client and all who will follow. Because you are using high, pure universal energy, your intentions must always come from your higher self (soul level) and not have any ulterior motives (lower ego issues). All humans have lessons to learn during their evolution on a global and personal level; however, they need to be put aside for your sessions.

Because you have spiritual gifts, when you use Reiki energy, your gifts will start to blossom and grow. Each individual's gifts are not the same. You'll be using your gifts (intuition) to guide where your hands need to be placed on a client for you to pass the light and energy of the universe.

Some masters will use their still minds to picture the areas needing attention on the body, while others will sense their feelings as guidance, and others will actually sense heat and cold in their hands for guidance.

The first lessons the Reiki student needs to learn are the main chakras (major energy centers of the body—spinning wheels of energetic light). This is necessary to make sure you clear the body properly, along with any specific physical areas you are drawn to.

It's best to keep your learning of the chakras very simple and basic, so your mind doesn't start chattering and take you out of a still, peaceful place.

The seven main chakras are as follows:

1. *Root*—bottom of the spine, color red, emotion of basic survival.
2. *Sacral*—midway between root and navel, color orange, emotions of creativity and sexual nature.
3. *Solar Plexus*—at the navel, color yellow, emotion of personal willpower.
4. *Heart*—middle of chest, color green, emotions of unconditional love and nonjudgment.
5. *Throat*—neck area, color blue, emotions of clear communication (physically and spiritually).
6. *Third Eye*—between eyebrows, color indigo, seat of intuition or psychic gifts.
7. *Crown*—top of head, color purple, your connection to your higher self, soul, the universe, God, Creator, or Great Spirit. Use what resonates with you personally in nonjudgmental form.

The chakras need to be cleared and balanced for your clients to live in emotional peace. Stressed-out emotions and thoughts will lead to disharmony (harmful state) in all areas of one's life. The goal of Reiki is for you to be living in a harmonious (no harm) state with yourself and the world around you. Peace must come from within yourself before you can experience it without (in the world around you).

The first aspect you need to address is that you are solidly grounded and your client is too. A good Reiki master or meditation teacher will be able to teach you various methods to achieve this state. You are in a physical body working with other physical beings; you should not be spaced-out or be using forms of transcendental meditation. You and your client should also avoid alcohol and/or drugs, to ensure you are grounded and remain clear at all times.

The next important step for the Reiki master to address is the four elements, which the client experiences at all times. These four elements need to be in balance for the client to be in his/her harmonious state. The four elements are as follows:

1. The physical body. This includes taking in all aspects that affect the body, including nutrition, exercise, fresh air, age, activities, rest, medical issues, and medications. The Reiki master must honor the laws of the medical profession and not diagnose or give advice. Reiki is a complementary healing tool to be used with honor and balance. It is best to remain silent through the greater part of the session and learn to listen (to your intuition, higher self, and the client). It's also best to phrase anything you pick up on as a question, simple and without interpretation or analysis.
2. The emotional body. This is the state where you need to be in a state of unconditional acceptance and nonjudgment yourself. Quite often clients will cry in an emotional release, and they need to be fully supported at that time. Emotions of anger, guilt, shame, regret, deep sorrow, and grief on many levels may surface. The Reiki master must be prepared to tell the client that a professional counselor may be a help if the client's emotions are overwhelming. Reiki masters must never assume they have enough life experience or expertise to heal another person's issues.
3. The mental body. This is the state where there need to be strong ethical boundaries between you and your client. As with the emotional body, if the client is overwhelmed

and under a great deal of stress, you must understand you are not a psychologist or counselor. Once again, remaining still and at peace is best, and not getting involved in the client's personal business is a form of respect.

4. The spiritual body. Every body has a spirit in it. In recognition of this, it's best to understand all spirits on this planet have a global and personal purpose here. Because we are individuals, we have our own unique paths and desires here. We have preferences and choices, with free will and different belief systems. This is where Reiki masters' intentions of unconditional love and nonjudgment really get tested. It is not the job of the master to change another being's faith, beliefs, or personal path.

In each of the four bodies there is a mixture of emotions and thoughts. The goal is to support the client with healthy thoughts and emotions. It is not the goal to analyze or change another person's experiences and lessons for personal growth. We are not here to *fix* one another. We are not meant to be carbon copies of each other. It's best to stay in gratitude and embrace and celebrate our differences. That is the true meaning of respect. If you stay in the mind-set that we are here to share and complement one another, then the law of cause and effect will easily keep your practice healthy and peaceful.

This is the area where the Reiki master gets tested the most. The universe is large and very diverse. Our current culture wants to know everything and can get caught up in arrogance, control issues, and manipulation. Reiki masters need to keep their intentions clear and clean on all levels for all beings and the planet. It is not our job to know or dictate how others live in harmony with their own personal lessons. On a higher level, each soul has come here to have specific lessons and experiences, and not all experiences are pleasant. Many humans are here to experience illness and disease, and eventually all beings face death. If you remain free of an arrogant attitude, you will realize you cannot cure everyone here. You can only support and help comfort others while they walk their own unique path.

The basic, simple goals for Reiki masters to remain clear, sacred conduits are as follows:

1. Always be honest.
2. Live with gentleness and compassion.
3. Show respect in all areas of one's life.
4. Practice humility daily.
5. Always be responsible for your actions.
6. Reach out with understanding.
7. Be still and peaceful.
8. Practice harmony with all beings.
9. Be willing to forgive.
10. Show goodwill in serving.
11. Share in balance.
12. Place honor first in all things possible.
13. Trust the universe with patience.
14. Reach out to help whenever possible.
15. Live with gratitude.
16. Wish well to all.
17. Keep your body and environment clean.

18. Focus on a healthy lifestyle.
19. Practice being nonjudgmental.
20. Let your heart guide your head.

One important note to keep in mind: Reiki is an experience, and experience cannot be truly learned in a few weekend courses. It has taken me decades to learn the truth and gain the authenticity to communicate this important information. Kindly remind your ego of this before you make the mistake of grandstanding. I have experienced a great number of unhealthy ego-bound teachers along the way. Although I learned important lessons, they were not peaceful or joyful. I will not be a hypocrite and say you are a master in weeks or even a few short years. In all humbleness, it takes a great deal of time before anyone can be called a master at anything in life.

The Reiki master needs to realize all good energy must radiate within to send good intentions outward. It is a daily discipline that takes focus, effort, and a loving attitude.

Please don't ever place your hands on another being without clear, clean energy backing them up. Please examine your own personal intentions as a daily, in-the-moment discipline at all times.

May the Creator of all creations find all who read this to be coming from honorable intentions. God bless and guide you with much love and light.

Thank you.

Helen White Wolf

MY CHAKRAS

Root chakra at the base of my spine, keeps me connected to ground;
Is bright red in color, continually spinning 'round and 'round.

Sacral chakra, a few inches higher, helps my creative juices flow;
It's orange in nature, where I get my passion, to keep on the go.

Solar plexus chakra, located at my navel, supplies personal drive;
Is the sun color yellow, and is the force behind my will to survive.

Heart chakra, in the middle of my chest, reminds me why I'm here;
It's green in color, helping me feel the sweet, gentle love of a deer.

Throat chakra, of course is the neck, it's the center to communicate;
Blue the color, truth is the goal, to staying real, not wind up a fake.

Third eye chakra, located at the brow, the place, of my sixth sense;
Strong indigo color, connection to spirit, helps keep me less tense.

Crown chakra, at the top of my head, where my God and I meet;
Violet color, soul is the game, fills me with light, and feels so sweet.

These are my seven major energy centers, on which I rely;
I must keep them clear and healthy, so I will not die.

Spin, spin, spin.

Helen White Wolf

CHAKRAS

NAME	COLOR	SOUND/NOTE	ENERGY
Root	Red	Uh/cup (C)	Grounding
Sacral	Orange	Ooo/you (D)	Creativity
Solar Plexus	Yellow	Oh/go (E)	Personal Power
Heart	Green	Ah (F)	Unconditional Love
Throat	Blue	I (G)	Communication
Third Eye	Indigo	A (A)	Intuition
Crown	Violet	E (B)	Connect to Divine

The 3 Bad *S*'s

1. Suffering

2. Sacrificing

3. Struggling

Helen White Wolf

Healthy Lifestyle

Spirit	**Physical**
Respect	*Reduce*
Responsibility	*Recycle*
Reverence	*Reuse*
Balance and Boundaries	
Intention and Integrity	
Live with Love	

LETTER TO BRIAN AND MATT

My Dear Nephews,

I have a very important story to tell you. I recently saw a church sign that said prayer doesn't need proof; it only needs practice. The story that I'm going to tell you is about how Angels prove every day that they exist, to show us God's love. All we need to do is be aware of how they reach out to us.

Every year around Christmas, the television station TCM plays a movie called *The Bishop's Wife*. In the movie, an angel tells the bishop that angels drop ideas in humans' heads, and the humans take credit for God's messages to them. The angel was smiling, full of love, as he was explaining how we take the angelic gifts for granted and boast that the ideas come from us. I watched the movie again this year, and then a miracle serendipitously happened days later.

Four years ago, a realtor sent me a refrigerator magnet about feelings, entitled, "Today I Feel." There are thirty different emotions and facial expressions on it. The frame that accompanies it is to help you acknowledge your different feelings on different days. I don't change the frame every day, but a few days after seeing the film I did. I had a thought that I should go over to the refrigerator and pick my feeling for the day. As I was changing the frame, I had another thought. Because I live all alone, I have no one to talk to anymore, so all my thoughts go straight to God and the Angels. My thought was it would be really nice for Brian and Matt to have one of these for themselves. That's all—just one thought and one sentence. Then I walked away from the refrigerator and didn't give it another thought.

I didn't tell any human about what I did or how I spoke to the angels in my thoughts. Exactly *two* days later, I received a letter in the mail. It had *two* magnets in it. I was surprised and impressed that the miracle took place in such a short time. I knew what I was supposed to do with the magnets, but the story was even more important for me to express.

So now that I've sent you the magnets from God's very loving Angels, I have two questions to ask you. The trick here is, *There's no wrong answer.*

Did I have the thought and the Angels answered it promptly? Or did the Angels drop the thought in my head because they wanted you to have these magnets? My conclusion is, the how, why, and where aren't the important part. It's the magic of the miracle and the proof that God speaks and listens to us through our thoughts. That's what is important.

The last part I'd like to tell you is that I believe God has a purpose for all of us. I watch every day as humanity forgets one another and those who are in need and alone. When humanity breaks my heart, I never lose faith that there is a God and Angels that love. And so every day until I take my last breath on Mother Earth, I will tell stories of God's beautiful Angels. This is what I believe is God's purpose for me. And I will be eternally grateful for how they touch us, show us that they always love, and listen to and remember us, while we take them and each other for granted.

I pray for you every day. And I am deeply honored that my Angels and your Angels allowed me to give you a gift from them and to tell a beautiful story about them.

God bless you always.

P.S. It would mean a great deal to me if you would save this letter and not throw it out. I can't explain why; it's just another one of my thoughts. Or is it? LOL

Helen White Wolf

A Tale to Tell

Since the beginning of time, humans have been learning.
Thousands of years have gone by; we're still yearning,
Searching and searching to find our deepest desire,
Everywhere we go, in our connections, igniting the fire.

Our souls choose many experiences and intense lessons,
Looking for harmony and the sweet methodical sessions.
We're not always sure that we chose the best direction;
Onward we'll trek, while trying out many a suggestion.

Two steps forward and one step back, still full of fortitude,
Determined to reach our goal, with a great deal of latitude.
As one scenario may look too dim, we rewrite the screenplay,
Opting out for a better conclusion, with our enemies at bay.

What have we been craving as we choose our inherent roles,
Traveling different journeys, from the prompting of our souls?
Passions fuel our every movement, from point A to point B,
Trying to manifest our desired destinies, and all that we can see.

History's full of repetition; the answer's always the same:
Our deepest soulful craving only goes by just one name.
It's the universal human goal, no matter what the game,
To love and be loved, and in this, there's never any shame!

Helen White Wolf